Time Management

*Increase Your Personal Productivity
and Effectiveness*

Harvard Business School Press | *Boston, Massachusetts*

Library of Congress Cataloging-in-Publication Data
Harvard business essentials: time management : increase your personal
productivity and effectiveness.
p. cm.—(Harvard business essentials series)
Includes bibliographical references and index.
ISBN 1-59139-633-6
1. Time management.   2. Scheduling.   I. Title: Time management:
increase your personal productivity and effectiveness.
II. Harvard Business School.   III. Series.
HD69.T54H374 2005
650.1'1—dc22
2004016538

Contents

Time
Management

Introduction

Irene looked up from her desk to see her colleagues packing up to go home. It was already 5:00 p.m. At the rate she was going she would be in the office until midnight. Staring down at her to-do list, she sighed in dismay. Three "must-do" tasks remained. What had she been doing all day, and why hadn't she gotten to these tasks?

She reviewed her day. She had spent the morning with Tony, her subordinate, talking about his monthly reports. During lunchtime she had replied to more than twenty e-mail messages. And all afternoon she had been consumed by a customer service request that should have been handled by somebody else. "But I wouldn't trust someone else to do it well," she told herself.

What was the point of all her to-do lists and careful planning if she wasn't getting to the work that she really needed to do?

Take a minute or two to reflect on your day at work. Was it like Irene's? Were you able to accomplish everything you had hoped to accomplish, or did you have to carry forward many important tasks from today's to-do list to tomorrow's? Did you feel rushed or compelled to cut corners? How about your subordinates? Did they complete all their assignments, or did they also come up short?

If you answered yes to these questions, you are in a time squeeze. Either you have too much work for the available time, or you aren't using your time effectively. In either case you have a time-management problem, and that problem will make your work life less fulfilling, less successful, and more stressful than it should be.

Time is a remarkable asset given to princes and paupers in equal measure. Every day contains twenty-four hours: no more and no less. And no matter how much we value it, there is nothing we can do to store it, to slow it down, or to put it into neutral while we prepare to use it. Time, as the saying goes, waits for no man. Time is also a wasting asset. It continually slips away, and we have no power to replenish our supply. The best thing we can do with time is to make the most of it. As Benjamin Franklin observed, "Dost thou love life? Then do not squander time, for that's the stuff life is made of."

Being time-sensitive people, we have surrounded ourselves with time-saving devices. Indeed, a substantial portion of human activity is dedicated to finding ways to accomplish the same things in less time. And so we have managed to cut travel time between Boston and London from the several weeks required by sailing vessels to eight hours via jet aircraft. We fill our workplaces with high-speed computers and blindingly fast assembly lines, and we concentrate on reducing the process time of doing almost everything. At home we surround ourselves with fast-cooking microwave ovens, heat-and-serve dinners, e-mail, and instant messaging.

But despite our efforts to make things happen faster, many of us find that we are always pressed for time. And, in a final irony, we spend a substantial percentage of our time working to pay for our many time-saving devices, such as automobiles capable of speeds up to 110 miles per hour that creep along, bumper-to-bumper, at 20 to 30 miles per hour a good part of the time. As early as the mid-1800s, Henry David Thoreau noted this odd trade-off, proclaiming that he could walk the thirty miles between Concord, Massachusetts, and the town of Fitchburg—and enjoy a country ramble—in less time than it would take to earn the train fare.

Humankind has been intensely interested in time and its passing since at least the time of the ancient Egyptians. Ancient people noted the sun's measured progress against the backdrop of the stars and used its movements to demarcate the year. The Mayan priests of Mesoamerica were especially dedicated to time. With remarkable precision they calculated its passing in days and years and used this knowledge to regulate agriculture and the rituals of daily life.

Until very recently, the broad sweep of time is what mattered. The seasons and the tipping points of the solar cycle—the solstice and the equinox—were the time measures that commanded people's attention. Measurement of time within any given day was imprecise and, until recently, of little interest. In his book *The Discoverers*, historian Daniel Boorstin described how Romans in the fourth century BC divided the day into two parts: before midday and after midday. We continue this division with a.m. (ante meridian) and p.m. (post meridian). This rough demarcation of time was apparently suitable for the pace of life at that time. Eventually, they used sundials and water clocks to mark the hours.[1]

The mechanical clockworks developed in Europe during the high Middle Ages added little more precision. Until the fifteenth century they merely tolled the hours. Simply knowing the hour was more than enough precision for most people. No one would say, "I have to deliver groats to the miller at 10:45 tomorrow morning and meet Sven at the salmon weir at 1:35." Minutes and seconds were of no particular interest; life was not paced to that level of rigorous measurement.

Things have changed. In the age of day-planners and personal digital assistant (PDA) schedulers, our working lives are increasingly assembled around fifteen-minute time blocks. We have only so much time for this and so much time for that, and little time to spare. This is a far cry from the lives of our ancestors of the eighteenth and nineteenth centuries, who had few laborsaving devices and yet somehow found time to listen to two-hour church sermons, keep diaries, build their own homes, and create beautiful quilts and folk art requiring hundreds of hours of painstaking labor.

James Gleick's interesting book *Faster: The Acceleration of Just About Everything* casts a sharp eye on our speed-driven culture and its obsession with real time, cycle time, nanoseconds, second-saving technologies, and the human problems of coping with all of them. "Can we stand the strain?" he asks, and he describes the small industry that has grown up around the treatment of "hurry sickness": mind-body workshops, stress-management seminars, and the growing popularity of meditation.[2]

On the business front, consultants George Stalk Jr. and Thomas Hout have given us *Competing Against Time*, an influential book that tells managers that speed—in customer response, new product development, and internal operations—is as strategically important as capital, differentiation, quality, and innovation. "Time-based competitors," they write, "are offering greater varieties of products and services, at lower costs and in less time than are their more pedestrian competitors. In so doing they are literally running circles around their slower competition."[3]

Time has likewise taken on greater military importance. Commanders now talk about the importance of "getting inside the enemy's decision cycle." In civilian language this means that if you can gather and process information, make a decision, and swing into action while the other side is still trying to understand the battlefield situation, you will have permanently captured the initiative—and the likelihood of victory.

Time management—the subject of this book—is a conscious attempt to control and allocate finite time resources. Concern with time and speed is most apparent in the workplace, where it now impinges on the lives of managers, technical professionals, and supervisors to the point of creating a minor industry of time-management seminars, day-planners, PDAs, and scheduling software. Effective time management has many benefits. These include a reduction in wasted time, mitigation of work overloads, and higher levels of personal productivity. Perhaps more important, time management ensures that the most important tasks get done.

The need for time management in the workplace is underscored by the frenetic pace of modern managerial life. In his classic article on the work of managers, business scholar Henry Mintzberg tells us, "Study after study has shown that managers work at an unrelenting pace, that their activities are characterized by brevity, variety, and discontinuity, and that they are strongly oriented to action and dislike reflective activities."[4] They spend almost no time sitting quietly in contemplation of the future. Instead, they are on and off the phone every few minutes, running into and out of meetings, and dealing with problems that appear out of nowhere. The fragmented, rushed, and unplanned life Mintzberg describes is more reactive and spontaneous than planned; it explains, in part, why many managers suffer stress and complain of never having enough time to do their jobs well.

Matters don't appear to get better as we move up the chain of command. As with other managers, the time available to CEOs is highly fragmented. Mintzberg found that the typical CEO allocates his or her time among various stakeholders as follows:

Directors	7%
Peers	16%
Clients, suppliers, associates	20%
Independents and others	8%
Subordinates	48%

So how does that compare with your time allocation on the job? Does the following sound familiar? Three long meetings—one a total time waster. At least a dozen phone calls. You've prepared for a working lunch with the boss, only to have her cancel at the last minute ("Let's reschedule for next Tuesday"). Two reports to write. Work on the upcoming presentation to senior management. Simmering conflict between two rival employees to deal with. And it's already time to start work on next year's budget. If this sounds like one of your workdays, then your day is like those of most other managers—filled with meetings, fragmented activities, interruptions, brushfires that need extinguishing, and business opportunities to exploit. There is little time to think, to plan, or to visualize the future you hope to create.

Handling many tasks would not be a problem except for one hard reality: There are only twenty-four hours in a day. Indeed, finding time to get all the work done is one of the biggest challenges managers face. And as rank-and-file employees are empowered to take greater control over their own operations, they too are facing the same challenge.

Time Pressure and Creativity

Time is one thing that every creative individual and creative team must have to achieve anything worthwhile. But how much time do they need? Does time pressure enhance or squash creativity? These are important questions for managers as they attempt to meet organizational goals with limited resources.

Academics have long studied the connection between time pressure and creativity. In general, these studies point to a curvilinear relationship between the two—that is, to a certain point, pressure helps; but beyond that point, pressure has a negative impact. Researchers Teresa Amabile, Constance Hadley, and Steven Kramer have reached some eye-opening conclusions. They point to instances where ingenuity flourishes under extreme time pressure—just as managers have always believed (or hoped)! They point, for example, to a NASA team that within hours came up with a crude but effective fix for the air filtration system aboard *Apollo 13*—a creative solution that saved the mission and its crew. On the other hand, these authors point to the Bell Labs teams that felt no such pressure but nevertheless created the transistor and the laser.

After studying more than nine thousand daily diary entries of people engaged in projects demanding high levels of creativity, Amabile et al. concluded that time pressure usually kills creativity. "Our study indicates that the more time pressure people feel on a given day," they write, "the less likely they will be to think creatively."

That's bad news for companies and managers, but it's not a lost cause. These researchers noted that time pressure affects creativity in different ways depending on whether the environment allows people to focus on their work, conveys a sense of meaningful urgency about their tasks, or stimulates or undermines creativity in other ways. For example, time pressure is not a creativity killer when people feel that they *are on a mission*, which is what the NASA crew undoubtedly felt. On the other hand, creative thinking under intense time pressure is less likely when people feel that they are *on a treadmill*—for example, when they suspect that their work is unimportant and when their work is highly fragmented (a typical manager's situation).

SOURCE: Teresa Amabile, Constance Hadley, and Steven Kramer, "Creativity Under the Gun," *Harvard Business Review,* August 2002, 56.

This book will help you make the most of your time and consequently increase your personal productivity and effectiveness. You'll learn to identify which jobs are most important—and least important—and deal with them according to their priorities. You'll learn to appreciate the difference between being efficient and being effective. And you'll discover how you can focus your time on the most critical tasks while avoiding time wasters.

Time management is the discipline of controlling your life through your use of the 168 hours that are available to you every week. Managing that time will force you to be explicit about what you value in your professional and personal life and will help you allocate your efforts accordingly. Mastering time management will help you balance the many pressures on your time and achieve your goals. That balance will help you avoid burnout and stress and will make you more productive at home and in the office.

What's Ahead

This book's treatment of time management is organized around eight chapters and several appendixes. The first three chapters focus on method. Chapter 1 is about workplace goals, the starting point of time management. If you identify and prioritize your goals, you will be off to a good start. Chapter 2 will help you understand how you spend the time at your disposal. As in household budgeting, it's hard to manage time effectively until you know your spending habits.

Are You Caught in the Time Trap? A Self-Test

- When you get into an elevator, do you automatically press the "close door" button rather than wait for it to close itself?

- Do you regularly recalibrate your wristwatch and clocks to the official time?

- Are more than 30 percent of your dinners either carry-out or heat-and-serve?

- Do you find yourself "multitasking" at work (e.g., skimming a report while a colleague is making a presentation to your group)?

- Are you too busy to take the midday walk you know you need to stay fit and healthy?

- Do you eat lunch at your desk while doing work or taking phone calls?

- Do you eat in your car while driving?

- If someone called with news that your father had been taken to the hospital with chest pains, your first thoughts would be about his welfare and getting right over to see him. Would your second thoughts be about the mess this will cause with your schedule?

If you answered yes to any of these questions, draw your own conclusions about the grip that time has on your life. For another self-diagnostic test, go online to the FranklinCovey site and try its Time Assessment Matrix (http://www.franklincovey.com/lifematters/index.html).

Chapter 3, "Scheduling Your Time," follows naturally and rounds out the discussion of method. It will help you make the most of day-planners, organizers, PC-based systems, and to-do lists.

The next three chapters address time-management challenges you regularly face at work. Chapter 4 describes the most common time robbers of contemporary organizational life: procrastination, travel, meetings, excessive e-mails, and so forth. Here you'll learn some practical tips for protecting your time from these bandits. Chapter 5 is a primer on delegating. For managers and supervisors, failing to delegate creates a huge time problem; conversely, effective delegating frees up time to plan, coach, and address other managerial functions. Chapter 6 addresses a touchy subject: the time-wasting boss. Bosses are supposed to get results through people, but some of them inadvertently fail in this because they waste the time of their subordinates by giving unclear directions, behaving as bottlenecks in the work flow, and so forth. This chapter will help you cope with the time-wasting boss.

Chapter 7 talks about the personal side of time. If you are like many people, you are as time-pressed at home as you are at work—with household chores, commitments to civic and family matters, and relationships, to name only a few. Fortunately, you can apply the methodology described earlier in the book to personal time management. This chapter will show you how.

Finally, chapter 8 describes things that companies can do to help people manage their time more effectively, both at work and at home. These approaches include the adoption of technologies that provide the benefits of travel without time wasted on commuting to distant locations. Other techniques include programs to enhance work–life balance and time-management training. Although time management is a personal responsibility, these are institutional arrangements that can help people be more successful in managing their time. Companies can make them happen.

The final section of this book contains items that will enhance your time-management skills:

- Appendix A contains a number of tools that can help you be more effective at managing your time. All the forms are adapted from Harvard ManageMentor® (HMM), an online product of Harvard Business School Publishing.

- Appendix B explains the use of a work breakdown structure (WBS). Managers use a WBS to deconstruct high-level goals into manageable tasks. This same methodology can be usefully applied to time management. See whether it works for you.

- Appendix C is a primer on effective meeting management. Meetings are so much a part of contemporary nonfactory work that everyone—both the people who lead meetings and those who participate in them—should understand good meeting practice. It is one of the best ways to make the most of time in the workplace.

- The glossary defines terms unique to time management. If you see a new term printed in italics, that's your cue that its definition can be found in the glossary.

- "For Further Reading" describes a set of books and articles that provide either much more material or unique insights into the topics covered in these chapters. If you'd like to learn more about any of the topics we've included in the book, these sources will help you.

The content of this book is informed by a number of books, articles, and online publications of Harvard Business School Publishing, in particular, articles in *Harvard Business Review,* and the Time Management module of HMM. Appendix A, "Useful Implementation Tools," contains worksheets from that module. Readers can also freely access worksheets, checklists, and interactive tools on the Harvard Business Essentials Web site: www.elearning.hbsp.org/businesstools.

The book also draws on a number of other published sources. Susan Alvey, a human resources professional, is owed special thanks for her insights into current time-management training practices.

Use Goals as a Guide

Your Compass to Personal Effectiveness

Key Topics Covered in This Chapter

- *The function of goals*

- *Critical, enabling, and nice-to-have goals*

- *Aligning goals at various levels*

- *Prioritizing your goals*

- *Mastering the dilemma of urgency versus importance*

- *How to break goals into achievable tasks*

- *Developing goals for subordinates and for your unit*

GOALS ARE THE starting point of effective time management. They act as a compass, pointing the way to the things on which you should be concentrating your time. If you identify your goals, you will know what is most important for you to accomplish on a daily, weekly, and monthly basis. Goals guide time management by helping you assign priorities to the many things that beg to be done.

This chapter will help you set goals and sort them in order of priority. It will also address the vexing problem of differentiating between what is urgent and what is important. Unless you are very careful, you can burn up most of your time on the urgent matters that must be done today even though these activities may do little to advance your goals. Finally, the chapter explains how to decompose goals into actionable tasks.[1]

Goal Setting

Goal setting is a formal process of defining outcomes worth achieving. When you set goals, you commit to outcomes that you can accomplish personally or through your team. By setting goals and measuring their achievement, you can

- focus on what is most important

- provide a unified direction for your team

- devote less energy to noncritical tasks

- avoid time wasters

- motivate yourself

- boost overall job satisfaction.

Goals differ in time frames and importance. Some goals are short-term, and others can be achieved only over months or years. In terms of importance, goals generally fall into one of three categories for individuals, operating units, and entire companies. These categories are critical, enabling, and "nice to have."

Critical Goals

Critical goals are essential to your success. They must be accomplished in order for your business or your unit to continue running successfully. For example, for a project manager, a critical goal might be to complete a two-year project on time and within budget. For a high-tech start-up company, achieving profitability within the time frame demanded by key investors might be a critical goal. These critical goals are end points.

Enabling Goals

Enabling goals create a more desirable business condition or take advantage of a business opportunity. They are important but fill a long-term, rather than immediate, need. In a sense, enabling goals facilitate the achievement of critical goals. They are not end points but bridges that carry us to them. Here is one example:

> *As the head of product development for a consumer goods manufacturer, Calvin has a goal to launch a continuous stream of successful and profitable new products. By agreement with his boss, the chief operating officer, Calvin aims to generate 30 percent of annual corporate revenues from products introduced in the previous five years. This is a critical goal. As an experienced R&D professional, Calvin understands all the planning, market research, and coordination required to turn out a steady stream of customer-pleasing products.*

Calvin also understands management rule 1: Managers get things done through other people. Consequently, he spends a substantial portion of his time—more than 50 percent—on issues that will make the people in his unit more effective in their work: training, finding the money to send people to scientific conferences, trying to retain the best people, visiting lead users of the company's products, and so forth. "I cannot always translate these activities into bottom-line results," he says, "but I know in my bones that they contribute to our mission."

Calvin is talking about enabling goals. For a company, an enabling goal might be the development and implementation of an effective pay-for-performance system. A unit's enabling goal might be to get the physical space it needs to do its work more efficiently. For a project leader, recruiting five top performers to a project team would be an important enabling goal. In this case, the project's objective is the critical goal; recruiting competent people to the project team is not a critical goal in itself but an enabler of the critical goal.

Nice-to-Have Goals

Nice-to-have goals make improvements that enhance your business. They usually involve making activities faster, easier, or more pleasant—for example, a new, easy-to-complete expense-reporting form, a more appealing cafeteria menu, or improved snow removal in the company parking lot. These are nice to have but will not supercharge your organization or its results.

Goal Alignment

Managers should create a set of cascading goals, beginning with company goals. Unit goals should, in turn, support company goals. Individual goals should then support the goals of the unit. These three levels of goals—company, unit, and individual—should be aligned and communicated to the point that an individual employee can say (without prompting), "Our company's goal is to _____. My department's contribution to that goal is to _____. And my part in this effort is to _____." In their valuable book *Align-ment*, George Labovitz and Victor Rosansky put it this way:

> *Imagine working in an organization where every member, from top management to the newly hired employee shares an understanding of the business, its goals and purpose. Imagine working in a department where everyone knows how he or she contributes to the company's business strategy. Imagine being on a team whose every member can clearly state the needs of the company's customers and how the team contributes to satisfying them.*[2]

Does this sound far-fetched—an ideal that sounds good in principle but not possible in practice? It isn't. Great companies are clear on their goals and on each employee's contributions to them. For example, Southwest Airlines employees—from flight crews to gate crews to baggage handlers—know that aircraft earn no money when they are sitting on the ground. The employees' goal is to get Southwest aircraft unloaded, reloaded, and back in the air as quickly and safely as possible. Everyone knows how he or she contributes to that higher goal.

Now consider your company. How explicit is management in defining and communicating its highest goals to employees? If you are a manager, how effective are you at spelling out goals to your unit and its individual members? Does each person understand the company's goals, its strategy for competitive advantage, and his or her part in the grand plan? The point to remember is simply this: If you do a good job of formulating and communicating goals, people will be in an excellent position to make the most of their time at work.

Take a minute to think about your personal workplace goals and those of your unit and your subordinates. Chances are that your workplace goals are identified in your official job description. If you lack an up-to-date job description, you and your boss should have mutually agreed on your goals during your most recent performance review. If you don't have a job description and haven't had a sit-down discussion with your boss, then shame on your boss. It is the boss's responsibility to work with every direct report in setting goals.

If your boss has been negligent, force the issue. Ask for a meeting to discuss your goals for the year and for the next six months. Reach an accord on which are critical, enabling, or simply nice to have. A mutual understanding of these goals is imperative. Don't settle for vague thoughts about what you should be accomplishing. To be effective guides to action, goals should have these characteristics:

- **Written down in specific terms.** Avoid vagueness in your goals. Vagueness will complicate your time-management problems.

- **Time-framed.** Does the goal need to be accomplished by the end of the week or the end of the year?

- **Measurable.** If you cannot measure progress toward your goals, you won't know when you've achieved them.

- **Important.** The goals you specify should lead to payoffs that you and the organization value.

- **Aligned with organizational strategy.** Unit goals should support the aims of the organization. Individual goals should support the aims of the unit.

- **Challenging and yet achievable.** Goals should make you stretch.

Remember too that what is good for you is good for your subordinates. They too should have critical and enabling goals. And those goals should have each of the characteristics just itemized: written, time-framed, measurable, and so forth. This is especially important when the organization is in a state of change, and when a subordinate is on a rapid trajectory toward workplace mastery.

As with you and your boss, the best time to discuss and reach agreement with subordinates on goals is during periodic performance appraisal meetings. Subordinates should be actively engaged in these meetings with you. It is important that they be part of the goal-setting process. After all, they are the ones who will have to pursue whatever goals are selected. As you work with subordinates on goal-setting for the coming six months or year, be sure that he or she (1) has the capacity to undertake the new goals and (2) understands their details and importance. Also, depending on the person's

Review Your Goals Periodically

As you work toward your goals, step back periodically and review them.

Are they still realistic?

Are they still timely?

Are they still relevant?

If the organizational or external environment has changed and reaching the goal will no longer create value, it is certainly appropriate, and indeed important, that you adapt. Ask yourself, "If I eliminated this goal, would anyone care?" On the other hand, you should not alter goals in reaction to obstacles such as personnel changes or a schedule slippage. When you need to change a goal, be sure to get buy-in from your team, your boss, and other involved groups before proceeding.

skills, this is the time to create a development plan (coaching, training, etc.) that will help the employee gain the needed capabilities.

Sorting Out Your Goals

Can you articulate your goals specifically? Which are critical? Which are enabling? Which are merely nice to have? Make a list of these goals using a worksheet like the one provided in figure 1-1, in which the owner-operator of a retail store has noted his goals for the year. (You'll find a blank version of this form in figure A-2.) Make a note of which are critical, enabling, and simply nice to have.

Then meditate for a minute or two on the content of the past few working days. Which goals commanded your time? The critical ones? The nice-to-have goals? Or was most of your time spent on activities that were unimportant to you but critical to someone else? If you're like most people, you will find progress toward your critical and enabling goals being crowded out by things that matter very little.

FIGURE 1-1

Prioritizing Your Goals

Goal	Priority	Comment
Obtain $500,000 in external financing on acceptable terms.	Critical	Essential for expansion to a second location. The company cannot grow without that second outlet.
Annual revenues from operations of $6 million and after-tax profits of $700,000.	Critical	In four years.
Train David to the point where he can take over operations at store #1.	Enabling	Within the next year. I cannot open a second store until David is ready to take over store #1 management.
Develop a low-cost and just-in-time supply chain.	Enabling	Could potentially cut cost-of-goods and inventory costs by $60,000 annually.
Improve health benefit program without adding significantly more cost.	Nice to have	Our health benefits are just barely competitive with other area retailers.
Improve the accounting system.	Nice to have	A better system would save time and give us more timely information for decisions and control.
Develop an e-commerce site.	Enabling	Our best option for increasing sales without adding more floor space.

The Urgent–Versus–Important Dilemma

One of the things that makes a mess of people's time allocations is a dilemma we all face: the matter of urgency. By definition, something that is urgent calls for immediate attention or action. But not every critical goal is urgent, and not every urgent matter is critical to your success. In fact, most critical goals are long-term and not momentarily urgent. Helen's critical goal is to build a retirement nest egg; she has twenty-one years to do it. Roberto is intent on obtaining $500,000 in external financing for his entrepreneurial business ("I can't expand to a second location without it"). But Roberto doesn't have to obtain this money immediately; he can continue operating his business at the current level until he finds the capital to expand. Polly is determined to complete her team's big project on time and on budget ("My boss and I have agreed to make this my top priority for the year"). Polly has intermediate milestones she must meet, but the first one is two months away and therefore cannot be defined as urgent.

Unfortunately, mundane but urgent tasks crowd out the time and resources we should allocate toward critical goals. This happens easily whenever our critical goals are long-term—that is, when there is no need to achieve them immediately. You may say, "I have six months to get that done, so I'll get these annoying, unimportant tasks done right now." Consider these examples:

- Helen's plan is to put $1,000 into her retirement fund every month, but her car needs some engine work right away. That will eat up this month's retirement contribution. She reasons, "I'll try to double up next month if I can afford it."

- Roberto knows that he should be networking with people who can lead him to an investor for his business—a critical goal. There is a luncheon scheduled for local entrepreneurs on Tuesday, and a Chamber of Commerce breakfast on Friday— both excellent networking venues. But there is no time for networking this week ("I have to file my tax return and meet with a contractor about remodeling our retail space").

- Polly cannot meet with her project team for several more days because the CEO has asked her to participate in the human resource department's all-day seminar on employee development. The boss admires her success in helping subordinates develop their careers and believes she'd make a contribution to the seminar. Polly also has a monthly report deadline to meet. The project team meeting will have to wait.

Notice that none of these "urgent" tasks has anything to do with the critical goals of Helen, Roberto, and Polly. Helen's automobile problem is important. She needs transportation. But building a retirement fund is a high-order goal. Similarly, Roberto has an urgent need to get his taxes filed on time; otherwise, he may be hit with a late fee. But filing on time will not bring him any closer to finding a financier who will invest in his business, and neither will meeting with a remodeling contractor. As for Polly, taking part in the seminar and getting a monthly report done on time may be high on someone else's lists of important matters, but not on hers. Participating in the seminar is nothing more than a pothole in the road toward completing her big project on time and within budget.

There is no escaping a certain number of urgent but unimportant activities. A colleague in another department desperately needs help from you in order to do her work. The person who signs your paycheck insists that you drop everything else and "get a list of our key customers in the southwestern region on my desk by four o'clock this afternoon." Money talks. The accounting department has lost the receipts you submitted with your last expense report. "Please contact the hotel and the car rental agency and ask for duplicate receipts," an e-mail says. The accounting department's problem isn't a big priority to you—but you do want to be reimbursed for your expenses. The tax authority has sent you a cryptic letter stating that your 2003 income tax return is being examined ("You must respond to this notice by contacting our examiner by noon of 21 May"). From your perspective, these are nothing but time wasters; they eat up time without bringing you closer to your goals, but you don't have much choice about them.

What urgent tasks are you facing this week? Make a list. Then compare that list of urgent tasks to your list of critical and enabling goals. Do you see anything resembling a match? Don't be surprised if most of the "urgent" issues on your list have nothing to do with your critical and enabling goals. In the absence of serious time management, it's easy for your days to fill up with urgent but unimportant activities. The same applies to many of the commitments we all make to others in the spirit of helpfulness. "Yes, I'll help you with that report," you tell a colleague. "Yes, I'll volunteer to sell raffle tickets for the school fund-raiser." Commitments like these keep us busy without necessarily bringing us closer to our higher goals. To be an effective time manager, you must discipline yourself to differentiate between what is urgent *and* important and what is simply urgent. When you recognize the difference, you'll know best how to allocate your time.

Perhaps the best way to reconcile the urgent-versus-important dilemma is to be conscious of the problem and to be deliberate about which unimportant but urgent task you choose to perform and which you will reject.

From Goals to Tasks

Recognizing and ranking your goals are essential if you're serious about making the most of your time. Unfortunately, many critical goals are so overwhelming that we cannot deal with them directly; instead, we must break them into manageable tasks and work on each of those tasks. It's like the old joke: "How do you eat an elephant?" The answer, of course, is that you eat an elephant by first carving it into bite-sized pieces. You must do the same with big, big goals.

We recommend the following four steps to using goals to manage time:

Step 1. Break each goal into a manageable set of tasks. Review each goal, and then list all the tasks required to achieve it. See figure 1-2 for an example.

Step 2. Prioritize. When you are satisfied that your list of tasks is complete, assign A, B, or C priorities to each one, with A representing the highest priority. The priorities you assign should reflect the importance of the goal that each task supports:

   A priorities involve your critical goals. They are tasks with high value and are of primary concern.

   B priorities involve your enabling goals and the most valuable of the nice-to-have goals. These are tasks with medium value and a high degree of urgency.

   C priorities are both urgent and nonurgent tasks with little value and little importance.

Step 3. Put the tasks in the correct sequential order. As you examine your tasks, you will notice that some need to be

FIGURE 1-2

Tasks and Time

Goal: Launch a series of internal training seminars—initially, two per month for a period of three months (a total of six). If well attended and judged effective, the series will be continued.

Task #	Activity	Time Estimate (Minutes)	Comment
1	Initial brainstorming meeting	60	Include Ramon, Harriet, Julie, and Peter
2	Second meeting: Determine subjects and speakers	75	Include all the above plus Fred
3	Brainstorm seminar site and internal promotion and communications	120	
4	Meet with each speaker individually	240	
5	Develop a communications package	180	Involve marketing
6	Supervise implementation	180	
7	Post-seminar evaluation	60	What worked and what didn't
8	Send each speaker a note of thanks and a small gift	60	
	Total time	975	Hours: 16.25

completed in a sequence, with each being more or less finished before the next task can begin. For example, a major report developed for senior management might have this sequence:

Gather data → Outline report → Write report → Circulate for comment → Revise → Submit report

Not all activities follow this neat linear sequence, which project managers refer to as a finish-to-start relationship. Some task sets, for example, exhibit a lagging relationship. Here, one task must await the start and partial completion of another, as shown in figure 1-3. Consider the development of a new computer system. The software developers must wait until some, but not all, of the hardware development is finished. After that point, much of their work can be done in parallel. Still other tasks are not dependent on the completion of any other particular tasks or can be done at any time before or after a particular stage is reached. Make a note of these relationships, and keep them in mind as you schedule your work.

Step 4. For A and B priority tasks—the ones you really intend to do—estimate how much of your time each task will require. That isn't always clear. But if you have completed a similar task before, you have the basis for a time estimate. If an activity is new to you, consult with colleagues, your manager, or others who may be able to help you with a time estimate. Then add a 10 to 20 percent cushion to allow for unanticipated

FIGURE 1-3

Task Relationships

In some cases, tasks logically have a linear relationship in which one task must be finished before another can start:

Other tasks have a lagging relationship:

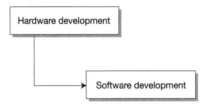

problems. You should also establish a deadline for the completion of each task or activity. For more complex activities, set up milestones along the way to track your progress. Figure 1-2 illustrates how one goal has been broken into its component tasks, with estimated times assigned to each.

After you have listed all the tasks and times, take another look. Try to identify tasks that you could reasonably delegate entirely or in part. For example, in figure 1-2, the manager might find that she can delegate most of task 3: "Brainstorm seminar site." She trusts her colleagues to handle that task without her. The same might be done with task 5, "Develop a communications package." Remember, the more tasks you can delegate, the more time you will have to concentrate on the most critical aspects of your goal.

For large goals that involve a team of other people, you should consider adopting the *work breakdown structure* (WBS) approach used by many project managers. A WBS is a planning routine that decomposes a project's goal into the many tasks required to achieve it. The time and money needed to complete those tasks are then estimated. See appendix B for a brief explanation of a WBS.

Unit Goals

This chapter has addressed your individual workplace goals. If you are a manager, you must also consider the goals of your unit. What should they be? You are surrounded by potential goal ideas. In a typical day, you probably think about how your unit can operate more smoothly, what new responsibilities it should be taking on, and how your staff can work better as a team. Each one of these areas can have associated goals. Your challenge is to sort through all potential goals and identify those that will create the most value for your unit and your organization.

On a regular basis (once or twice a year), review your unit's diverse activities and look for opportunities to make a greater impact.

Call your team together and brainstorm possible goals by asking questions such as these:

- What initiatives need to be completed to ensure success?

- What standards are we striving for?

- Where can we have the greatest positive impact on productivity and efficiency?

- Are customer requirements for our products and services changing? How can we respond?

Don't allow worries about constraints or execution limit your brainstorming. Instead, make a list of what people see as their top concerns. Then work as a group to narrow the list to the goals that people see as most important. As you do, make sure that these goals are aligned with the strategy and goals of the company as a whole.

Whether you follow this methodology rigorously or simply think about your goals and their priorities, make goals your starting point for time management. Goals will then guide all your subsequent thinking and doing.

Summing Up

- Goals are the starting point of effective time management. Everything else should follow from them. Don't expect much from time management until you've identified your goals.

- Goals can be categorized—in order of importance—as either critical, enabling, or nice to have.

- Seek alignment between company, unit, and individual goals.

- To be effective guides to action, goals should be written in specific terms, time-framed, measurable, important, aligned with organizational strategy, and challenging and yet achievable.

- As you work with a subordinate on goal-setting, be sure that he or she (1) has the capacity to undertake the new goals and (2) understands their details and importance.

- Urgent but relatively unimportant tasks can easily consume time that you should spend on critical and enabling goals. Learn to identify those tasks for what they are.

- Critical goals are often very large in scope and thus difficult to address. In these cases, break goals into their component tasks and address each in the right order.

- Operating units should have their own goals.

2

How You Spend Your Time

Where Does It Go?

Key Topics Covered in This Chapter

- *Using an activity log to document how your time is spent over several days*

- *Analyzing log data and finding the causes of bad time-management practices*

- *Making a habit of good time-management practices*

CHAPTER 1 ADVISED YOU to use goals as a compass in guiding your use of time. That's hard to do if you don't give some thought to how you currently use your time. Taking control of your time is much easier if you understand how you are currently spending it. With your household budget, you cannot plan and control future spending unless you understand your current spending habits. The same thing applies to your current time-spending habits.

How much of your time are you now spending on paperwork? In meetings? On the telephone? In travel? In idle Web surfing? If you get an accurate picture of how you are spending your time, you'll know where you are wasting it and how to use it more effectively.

This chapter will show you how to develop an activity log, the primary tool for determining how your time is being spent. This would be a tedious chore if it were not such an eye-opener. After you create one of these logs, you are likely to say, "No wonder I never have time to work on important business—I've been wasting so much of it."

Create and Use an Activity Log

If you were asked to write a chronology of your workday yesterday, you'd surely remember the important things you did and approximately how much time you spent doing them. "Well, let's see. I started the day by answering e-mail. That took a few minutes. There was a meeting at 9:15, which lasted until 10:30 or so. I then made some phone calls and left early for a meeting with a salesperson from one of our suppliers . . ."

How much do you remember about yesterday? Your recollections may be fairly accurate about scheduled meetings because they usually begin at an appointed hour, but it's easy to overlook time spent on other bits and pieces of work, especially coffee breaks, dealing with e-mail, and so forth. To understand your time-spending patterns, you need to create a written record—an *activity log*—for at least three days, preferably for an entire week. Ideally, the log will cover typical days—not days that include an unusual amount of travel, a multiday sales meeting, and the like. Be sure to log every activity as you do it; in that way, you won't overlook anything, particularly the many brief activities and time wasters that are part of most people's days.

Figure 2-1 is a sample activity log for one person's workday. Note that she has recorded even minor things, such as waiting for her computer to boot up, tidying her desk, and taking bathroom breaks. She has made a log entry every time she changed activities. These small things add up during the day but would likely be forgotten if she tried to complete the log from memory at day's end. Try this yourself tomorrow, beginning from the time you walk through the door of your workplace until the moment you leave for home. Be as accurate as possible in recording the length of time spent on each activity. Do not leave out anything.

As you complete each line of the activities section, try to label it by specific categories such as "e-mail," "paperwork," and so forth whenever possible. Categorizing your activities will make it easier to analyze your log later. An office worker's activity categories, for example, might include the following: e-mail, Internet, phone, paperwork, planning, preparation, meetings, visitors, and travel.

FIGURE 2-1

Sample Daily Activity Log

	Activity	Minutes Used	Priority
8:42	Waited for computer to boot up	3	C
8:45	E-mail: check and respond	15	B
9:00	Break: Coffee room; chatting	9	C
9:09	Wait for meeting; tidy desk	6	C
9:15	Meeting: Product launch team	60	A
10:15	Break: Coffee; personal e-mail; bathroom	15	C
10:30	Phone: External S Heming, Confirm lunch	12	B
10:42	Phone: Internal D Gertz, eng. dept	8	B
10:50	E-mail: Respond to Bill	3	C
10:53	Internet—check weather, news	7	C
11:00	Prepare: for lunch meeting	8	B
11:08	Meeting: Bonus plan discussion	32	C
11:40	Travel: to off-site lunch meeting w A Davis	120	B
1:52	E-mail: send and respond	12	C
2:04	Phone: return voice messages	11	C
2:15	Visitor: summer intern asking directions	8	C
2:23	Visitor: D. Horowitz asked about project	5	A
2:28	Paperwork: begin monthly project report	4	B
2:32	E-mail: incoming	3	C
2:35	Paperwork: resume project report	12	B
2:47	Break: Bathroom; get coffee	10	C
2:57	Prepare: Gather material for meeting	3	B
3:00	Meeting: budget review	75	B
4:15	E-mail: send and respond	11	B
4:26	Internet: check news	4	C
4:30	Plan: check/adjust calendar for project work	10	A
4:40	Paperwork: resume project report	10	B
4:50	E-mail: outgoing, project related	10	B
5:00	To home		

Rating Travel

Let's suppose that you have spent half a day traveling to an important meeting halfway across the country. The subject of that meeting represents one of your critical goals: It has an *A* priority. In filling out your activity log, you put an *A* next to the hours spent in that meeting. But what about the four hours you spent getting there by airplane and taxi? Do they rate an *A* because they are associated with the important meeting?

Our answer is no. That time should be rated for what it actually produced. If you used part of that time to write a report or prepare for the meeting, it should be rated accordingly. Time spent looking out a taxi window or watching an in-flight movie would have to be rated as *C*, a time waster. Dealing with travel time in this way provides a reminder of the cost of travel, even when it supports a high-priority end.

After you have logged your activities, assign a priority to each one, based on your critical goals, enabling goals, and nice-to-have goals as described earlier. Remember:

- *A* priorities involve your critical goals. They are tasks with high value and are of primary concern.

- *B* priorities involve enabling goals—activities that indirectly support your critical goals. These are tasks with medium value and a high degree of urgency.

- *C* priorities include both urgent and nonurgent tasks with little value.

Analyze Your Activity Log

After you have finished the priorities column, examine the log to identify patterns of time use. Are you burning up lots of time on paperwork, coffee breaks, and talking with unscheduled visitors?

Perhaps you spend a lot of time Monday mornings on the telephone, or you tend to have unexpected visitors after lunch. You may find that meetings cluster late in the week.

Ultimately, you must ask, "Does this use of time match my key responsibilities and goals?" Spending most of the day on telephone calls may be fine if you're in sales, but perhaps not if you work in accounts payable. Conversely, salespeople who spend most of their time on paperwork and little of it talking with customers would be misusing their time.

Pay particular attention to the priority column of your log. How much of your day is spent on *A*- and *B*-priority activities? Hopefully, most of it. There will always be some *C*-priority activities in your log, but they should be a very small part of your day.

Now look for the payoff. You don't want to spend 50 percent of your time on activities that have minimal payoff in terms of your responsibilities and goals. Perhaps you can eliminate or delegate some of these minimal payoff activities. For example, the person who filled out figure 2-1 spent thirty-two minutes attending a meeting on the company bonus plan, a *C* priority for her. She should ask herself, "Do I really need to attend these bonus plan meetings given my responsibilities and priorities?"

Now go after the time wasters. To make them more obvious, mark them on your log with a yellow highlighter. If you see lots of yellow, you'll know that there is plenty of room for improvement. Then you can develop ways to avoid them. For example, the person whose workday is represented in figure 2-1 has spent 123 minutes on *C*-priority tasks. That's not bad, but it points up opportunities for improvement. On the other hand, only 75 minutes of the entire day were involved with *A*-priority tasks, signaling a potential problem. Why is she spending only an hour and fifteen minutes each day on top-priority work?

From Analysis to Change

Documenting your time use and analyzing your findings are the necessary first two steps in time management. They are necessary but not sufficient. A third active step is required before you can improve: You must plan for change.

If you've been around product or service operations for any length of time, you're probably familiar with a methodology called process improvement. If you haven't, here's a brief explanation. Business processes convert inputs to outputs; for example, an automobile assembly process converts a collection of supplier-built parts into a finished vehicle. It makes no difference whether we're talking about processes that convert steel bars into automobile camshafts or processes that turn loan applications into formal acceptance or rejection decisions.

Processes may be efficient or inefficient. The output may meet rigorous speed or quality standards, or it may fall short; for example, if the camshaft process produces substantial variation in output, resulting in lots of scrappage, the process is out of control. The people who conduct process improvement do the two things we described earlier with respect to time management: They gather data about what is happening, and they analyze it, looking for problems. Then they go two steps further: They seek the causes of process problems, and they take action to correct or eliminate the causes of the problems.

You can apply this same methodology to time management. You've seen how you can use an activity log to gather and analyze data to identify problems. It's now time for the final two corrective steps.

Seeking the Causes of Time Mismanagement

After your analysis has identified bad time-use patterns, it's time to find the causes. Ask and answer tough personal questions such as the following. Be honest with your answers.

Q: Why am I spending so much time in low-value meetings?

A: I'm afraid that people won't think of me as a team player if I decline meeting invitations.

Q: What explains the amount of time I'm frittering away on unscheduled visitors and incoming phone calls?

A: I'd feel rude if I told people that I didn't have time to talk with them. Also, I leave my door open and pick up the phone whenever it rings.

Q: Why do I spend so much time on e-mail and the Internet?

A: Some of it is business related, but half of the e-mail is personal, and much Web surfing is strictly a way of procrastinating.

This type of inquiry will bring you to the causes of wasted and misallocated time and will prepare you for the final step.

Correcting the Problems

Poor time management is essentially a behavior problem. It helps if you recognize the problem and understand its causes, but this will get you only so far. The best way to correct the problem is to develop more desirable habits of behavior. This is exactly what one of America's founders, Benjamin Franklin, did in shaping his own life.

As a young man making his way in the world of colonial Philadelphia, Benjamin Franklin identified thirteen virtues whose regular practice, he believed, would make him a better and more successful person. They included temperance, silence, order, resolution, frugality, industry, sincerity, and humility. A systematic man, Franklin knew that simply writing the virtues down on a piece of paper and setting that paper on his desk would have little effect on his day-to-day behavior. Long before psychology and behavior modification became formal disciplines, he understood that people do not change by thinking; they change by doing—that is, by practicing a new behavior.

So Franklin set himself to a self-improvement program in which he concentrated on practicing each of the virtues for one week before moving on to the next. Each week of practice, he believed, would create a habit of behavior that would stick with him over time, making the thirteen virtues part of his manner of living and dealing with others. He even kept a notebook in which he recorded every lapse of virtuous behavior as a way of keeping track of his own progress.

One of Franklin's virtues—industry—was an eighteenth-century version of what we now call time management: "Lose no time; be always employ'd in something useful; cut off all unnecessary actions."[1]

Franklin's approach to the thirteen virtues is not simply a quaint story. It recommends itself as a method for correcting the bad time-management habits found in activity log analysis. The method has the added benefit of tackling the problem through a series of small, achievable steps instead of trying to fix everything at once. So if your e-mail use and Web surfing are causes of poor time usage, spend a week consciously taming them. After you have them under control, move on to the next bad habit.

If you are like most people, the acts of logging and analyzing your actual time-spending behavior over several days will reveal that you have more time available than you realized—if only you can eliminate time-wasting activities and spend less of your day on routine things that contribute little to your success. But remember what Franklin understood intuitively: that simply recognizing a problem is not a solution. Behavior does not change by thinking but by doing—by practicing a new, more effective behavior over and over again.

Summing Up

- The first step of time management is to understand how you currently spend the time you have. You can best accomplish this by keeping an activity log over three to five days.

- It's simpler to analyze an activity log if you label each activity with a general category (e.g., travel) and assign it a goal-related priority.

- The next step after activity analysis is to find the cause of time mismanagement.

- The final step is problem correction. The best way to correct the problem is to develop more effective habits of behavior by repeatedly practicing the effective behavior until it becomes a natural response (a habit).

3

Scheduling Your Time

Start with Your Priorities

Key Topics Covered in This Chapter

- *Using lists and planners*

- *Building a schedule around key priorities*

- *Using a daily to-do list*

- *Scheduling if you have an unstructured job*

I F   Y O U ' V E   F O L L O W E D   the advice of the first two chapters, you clearly understand your goals and their priorities: which are critical, which are enabling, and which are simply nice to have. You have also analyzed your time-spending patterns using an activity log for three to five days. That analysis will indicate how much time you typically devote to various activity categories: paperwork, directing subordinates, attending meetings, planning, traveling, and so forth.

After you've identified and prioritized all the tasks for which you are responsible, you need to deal with them systematically. The best approach is to use a schedule, a written commitment to accomplish tasks within a specific time. A schedule allows you to visualize time resources and your plan for allocating them. You can see at a glance time blocks in which you are committed or uncommitted. You can also see whether priority tasks are being crowded out by less important ones. *A*- and *B*-priority tasks should dominate the schedule, with *A* tasks given preference. You may allocate a small portion of the time to *C*-level tasks and urgent but unimportant activities that you cannot delegate or escape.

Scheduling Tools

There are plenty of scheduling tools available. If you go into any office supply store, you will see stacks of many different types available for the coming year. All of them promise to make you better organized and thus more productive. These products include the following:

- To-do lists

- Appointment calendars

- Daily and weekly planners

- Scheduling software and hardware (for example, PC-based calendars and personal digital assistants)

Many organizations have calendar-scheduling software tools such as Microsoft Outlook. These allow you to maintain your schedule on your personal computer and, if company PCs are networked, to view the calendar availability of your colleagues. Networked scheduling makes it much easier to find times when colleagues have uncommitted periods when they can meet or collaborate on tasks. A company interviewed for this book found this type of software so useful that it was able to eliminate one full-time staff position. Before installation of the software, that person did nothing but coordinate meeting times for other employees. Outlook includes its own version of a to-do list. FranklinCovey, a company that offers time-management training based on principles expounded in Stephen Covey's popular book *First Things First*, has developed add-on tools that integrate its planning methods into Microsoft Outlook to help knowledge workers focus on their priorities and to help working teams become more effective.

Use these tools if they are available. But keep in mind that scheduling is personal; if the tools available at your firm do not fit your personal style, seek others that do.

Building Your Schedule

As you build a schedule, always begin with *A*-priority tasks. These should have first call on your time. By scheduling these first you will accomplish two important time-management results: You will have

Available-to-Promise

Not sure whether you have the capacity to take on additional responsibilities or projects? Here's a planning tool that can help you.

Manufacturers use master scheduling techniques to match their supply of parts and production capacity with their demand for completed orders. When properly used, these techniques ensure that the right number and the right type of parts converge with available production capacity to let the company fill customer orders on time.

Among the techniques of master scheduling is a tool called available-to-promise (ATP). This tool, usually set up on an electronic spreadsheet, reveals at a glance the supply of production capacity available in any given time to accept additional order demand. This same tool can be adapted to an individual's work schedule.

Consider this example. Carmen, a freelance writer, is currently working with five clients on as many books and articles. She has set up an available-to-promise tool in Excel, indicating her total work capacity (supply) in days for each of the next six months. Her estimate of the number of days required to satisfy each client's demand in each month is also indicated. The tool calculates the total work demand for each month and subtracts that number from each month's total number of working days (total capacity). The result is the number of days Carmen has available to take on new business in any month. In this example, Carmen plans to work twenty-six days in July and has already committed twenty-four days to various clients, leaving two left "to promise" to whoever requires her services (see table 3-1).

time to deal with your most important responsibilities, and you will leave much less room for time wasters to creep in. So, as a first step, insert your *A*-priority tasks into appropriate time slots over the coming days, weeks, or months. Then accommodate your *B*-priority tasks using the remaining time.

TABLE 3-1

Available-to-Promise

Project	Jul	Aug	Sep	Oct	Nov	Dec
Client A	1		6			
Client B		10				
Client C	4	3				
Client D	7		4	12		
Client E	12	10	7	10		
Total Demand	24	23	17	22	0	0
Total Capacity	26	25	19	25	24	20
ATP	**2**	**2**	**2**	**3**	**24**	**20**

As you set up the schedule, keep in mind that your days undoubtedly have periods of high and low energy. For example, afternoons are periods of low energy for many people, particularly immediately after lunch. If this is your experience, schedule important work or activities that require creativity and energy in the morning, when you are most alert and energetic. Schedule routine tasks—handling e-mail, reading reports, and so forth—during low-energy periods.

Here are a few important tips for completing your schedule:

- **Schedule only part of your day.** This is crucial for managers and becomes more important as you move into the higher management echelons. Leave some time open to deal with crises, opportunities, the unexpected, and that tried-and-true approach to management: walking around. If you leave unscheduled time on your calendar, however, jot down the *A*- and *B*-level tasks you will do *if* crises and unexpected events do not soak up your free time.

- **Schedule your highest-priority work first.** This is your best assurance that important tasks will not be crowded out by urgent but unimportant work. Fill in remaining times with lower-priority tasks as your calendar permits.

- **Avoid back-to-back meetings if possible.** You need time to process the information obtained in each meeting and to execute the action items they produce.

- **Consolidate tasks such as e-mail, paperwork, and phone calls when possible.** For example, set aside 9:00 to 9:30 a.m. for these tasks and again at 4:30 to 5:00 p.m. Consolidating tasks usually reduces the total time required to do them by eliminating start-up and *switching* costs (the time it takes to get started again after you're interrupted).

- **As the week progresses, move uncompleted priority tasks to future open times.** If no open times are immediately available, bump lower-priority tasks. Always put the most important things first.

- **Try scheduling backward.** Determine the time you have that day and then work backward. Put in the most important things first.

If you find yourself unable to complete all high-priority tasks as originally scheduled, make a mental note of what prevented you from doing so. Did you underestimate the time needed to get the job done? Did you procrastinate or allow interruptions to steal part of that time? Did you leave too little time available for unanticipated problems? As you answer these questions you are likely to see a pattern. Rework future portions of your schedule to reflect what you have learned. Like everything else, scheduling should be a matter of continuous improvement over time.

After you have created your schedule, keep it in sight. A wall or desk calendar should always be in view; a computer-based calendar should always be open on your desktop. Check your progress throughout the day to ensure that you are on track.

Note: It is important to periodically review the effectiveness of your scheduling technique. Appendix A contains a helpful checklist that will take you through a set of self-diagnostic questions. These will help you improve scheduling on a regular basis.

Working with a To-Do List

A to-do list is one of the simplest and most commonly used scheduling tools. It captures all the tasks you need to complete on a given day in one eye-catching format. Many people use a to-do list in combination with a weekly or monthly schedule. Many day-planners and computer calendars have to-do lists built in. An effective to-do list includes the following:

- Meetings you are scheduled to attend—and when

- Decisions you must make

- Calls you must make or expect to receive

- Memos, letters, and e-mails you must write

- Unfinished *A*- or *B*-priority business from the previous day

One of the virtues of a to-do list is that it allows you to break down your tasks into specific activities. For example, while your day-planner schedule might direct you to "return phone calls" on Tuesday between 3 p.m. and 4 p.m., your daily to-do list would identify each person you need to call, as in the following list:

Do These Today

Work on budget, 10–noon

Team meeting, 1–2 p.m.

Return phone calls, 3–4 p.m., to:

- Herb—performance appraisal meeting
- Juanita—salary review
- David K.—his late shipment
- Clarissa—her monthly sales

Finalize decision on London trip by 5

Create your to-do list either at the end of the day for the next day or at the very beginning of the day in question. Make a ritual of this activity. Doing so will, in itself, help you make a habit of time management.

As you compile your list, be realistic about how many things you can accomplish in a day. A rule of thumb is to include half the number of things you think you can do. That may seem pessimistic, but try this rule for a few days and make adjustments moving forward. And be exceptionally diligent about keeping urgent but unimportant and low-priority tasks off the list unless someone in authority has required you to do so. It's very tempting to tell yourself, "I'll put all these unimportant items on my list and quickly get them out of my hair. Then I can get down to the important business." If you do that, you will have given time wasters priority over tasks that really matter. And if those unimportant tasks take longer than expected, you will have shot yourself in the foot. So keep them off the list.

Finally, cross each task off your list as it is completed. That is bound to give you a real sense of satisfaction. Review the list at the end of the day. Were any high-priority items left undone? If they were, they will have to be rescheduled—but first ask yourself *why* you failed to complete them as planned.

Did you fail to schedule sufficient time for these tasks?

Is some form of unconscious avoidance involved here?

If you answered yes to that last question, then ask yourself why you avoided those tasks. Were you afraid that you'd fail to do them well? Would completion of those tasks have involved a personal conflict you'd rather avoid?

Get to the bottom of the problem first, and then reschedule all the high-priority tasks that remain on your to-do list.

The Weakness of Scheduling Systems

You may be thinking, "This is all very sensible, but my work and the problems I must address are too changeable and too undefined to fit neatly into a scheduling system." And there is a good chance that you are right. Prioritizing tasks and using a day-planner to handle them are extremely useful when jobs are highly structured and tasks are clearly defined. These tools are progressively less useful, however, as your duties become less structured and more opportunistic, something that often happens as people move up the ladder to professional, managerial, and executive positions, as shown in figure 3-1.

Generally, people's jobs become less structured as they take on higher levels of managerial responsibility. Time allocations grow more fragmented as the breadth of their responsibilities expands. Every day brings problems and opportunities that were not in the script, wreaking havoc with day-planners. Consider this hypothetical case:

> *As owner-manager of DaveCo Systems, David had his day nicely mapped out. His morning calendar was filled with meetings, first with the programming group and then with sales. He was scheduled to have lunch with a candidate for the open operations manager position, followed by a budget work session with the CFO. To fill out the day, David planned to tag along with one of the salespeople on a visit to a local company between three and five.*

FIGURE 3-1

Organizational Rank and the Structure of Work

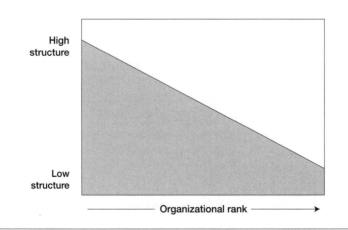

The second of his morning meetings had just begun when someone poked his head through the door to say, "David, I apologize for interrupting, but you have an urgent phone call." And it was urgent. Two employees had been involved in an auto accident en route to a customer site. Both they and another driver were in the hospital. David's tidy schedule was shot to pieces.

How can a priority and scheduling system deal with developments like this one? The answer is that a tightly structured system cannot deal with ambiguity and unpredictability—characteristics that go hand in hand with high-level professional and managerial work. What's needed is a scheduling method that mirrors the flexibility required for success in that type of work.

Perhaps 90 percent of what has been discussed in chapters 1 and 2 about making goals, prioritizing tasks, and scheduling applies to high-level professionals and executives. Lacking clear goals, managers cannot steer themselves nor their subordinates in the right direction. If they do not prioritize, they will spend too much time on tasks that don't bring them closer to their goals. And without a schedule, every day's work is ad hoc and reactive. So the CEO needs the same time-management tools as the lower-level manager, the salesperson, and the engineer. The only difference is that the CEO needs more flexibility in applying these tools. Flexibility takes these forms:

- More free time built into daily schedules

- Only the most important critical tasks and deadlines entered in schedules two or more weeks down the road

- A greater willingness to bump scheduled tasks as opportunities present themselves

Greater flexibility will not make a person's day any less full, but it will ensure that there will be time for the things that matter most.

This and the previous two chapters have described a practical method for managing time in the workplace. The next two go beyond that method to explain practices you can use to unburden yourself of tasks that soak up time and diminish your productivity.

Summing Up

- Networked PCs with scheduling software allow users to easily coordinate employee schedules for meetings and collaborative work.

- Schedule top-priority activities first; fill in lower-priority work in the remaining time.

- Avoid overscheduling your time. Leave some time open to deal with unexpected crises, opportunities, and so forth.

- Consolidate tasks such as e-mail and paperwork to reduce start-up and switching costs.

- Use a to-do list to capture all the tasks you need to complete on a given day.

- Schedules and day-planners work well for people whose jobs are highly structured, and less well for people, particularly higher-level managers, whose work is fragmented. People with less structured jobs can make the most of time-management tools by building more free time and flexibility into their schedules.

4

Time Robbers

How to Defeat Them

Key Topics Covered in This Chapter

- *The three causes of procrastination and how to conquer them*

- *How to avoid taking on more responsibilities than you can handle*

- *The danger of assuming subordinates' problems and responsibilities*

- *Time-smart travel*

- *Dealing with the twin monsters: e-mail and paperwork*

- *Making the most of meetings*

- *The cost of switching from task to task*

THE ABILITY OF managers and employees to allocate their time effectively is frustrated by a number of factors. Unanticipated crises must be dealt with immediately. Demanding customers call for more attention. The sudden illness of a coworker means that his teammates must adjust their workloads to pick up the slack.

Factors such as these may be beyond your control. Many time-management problems, however, originate in individual behavior and habits, both of which can be corrected, as described earlier. This chapter considers several self-imposed time robbers and explains how you can defeat them.

Procrastination

Procrastination is the habit of delaying or putting off doing something that should be done now. We all procrastinate to some extent, both at home and at the office. The result is that high-priority tasks are postponed or, worse, never completed. And all the while, procrastinators feel guilty or feel as though they have a monkey on their backs.

There are generally three reasons for procrastination:

- The task is unpleasant or uninteresting.

- You fear failure.

- You don't know where to begin.

Unpleasant and Uninteresting Tasks

Some of the important things we must do are either unpleasant or uninteresting. Consider this scenario:

> *Sandra knows that she must confront Helen, her subordinate, about Helen's habit of getting to work five to ten minutes late every day. That behavior cheats the company and sets a terrible example for other employees, who are very aware of Helen's tardiness—and Sandra's laxity in dealing with her. Nevertheless, Sandra hasn't done anything about the problem.*

What's going on here? Why is Sandra allowing this problem to continue? It is possible that her procrastination is an unconscious way of avoiding an unpleasant task. Few people, including managers, enjoy telling others that they are doing something wrong. Many people, in fact, shrink from personal confrontation. They do the same with tasks they find uninteresting.

What unpleasant but important tasks have you failed to address this week? Did you spend your time on unimportant matters simply to avoid those unpleasant tasks? One clue to this habit may be found in your day-planner or daily to-do list (assuming that you use them). Take a look at the uncompleted tasks that remain on your list at the end of each day. Why were other tasks completed and these weren't? Did you find them unpleasant or uninteresting?

Here are some cures for this form of procrastination:

- If it's feasible to delegate unpleasant tasks, do so. Tasks that are unpleasant to you might not be unpleasant to someone else.

- If you cannot delegate those tasks, admit to yourself that you are procrastinating because you find them unpleasant. Doing this requires an ability to get outside your own skin and look at the situation objectively. This is difficult but is the first step to saying, "Yes, this is unpleasant, but I'll just have to bite the bullet and do the job."

- Procrastination usually produces guilt and internal dissatisfaction. So if you catch yourself avoiding certain jobs, think about the relief you'll feel after you've addressed the unpleasant task. That good feeling may be a sufficient incentive to get you moving.

- Schedule the unpleasant task in a way that will make it difficult or impossible to turn back. For example, Sandra should schedule a meeting with Helen early the next day. She should then follow up with a reminder e-mail containing this subject line: "About our starting time." There will then be no turning back.

After you have completed the unpleasant task, you will feel a sense of relief and may even ask yourself, "Why didn't I take care of that business right away?"

Fear of Failure

Fear of failure can be another cause of procrastination. We all try to avoid failure, so if it's unlikely you can successfully complete a task, you're naturally tempted to avoid it. Consider this scenario:

Jim and his boss, Ron, were having lunch together in late January. "The department performed very well this past year," Ron began, "but it will have to do even better this year, given the goals we've been assigned." He went on say that he wanted Jim to form a task force to find ways of improving the department's work processes. "I want that task force to find ways to operate faster and cheaper without any reduction in quality. And I'd like a report in three months."

Jim was flattered that Ron had asked him to lead an important department initiative. But he had reservations. The people he would have to recruit to the task force didn't particularly like him, perhaps because he was new to the company, perhaps because he was younger. Jim had never had much success in collaborating with those people. What would happen if they simply ignored him? "There's a high likelihood of failure here," he told himself.

Now, several weeks later, Ron asks Jim, "Do you have anything to report on work process improvement yet?"

"Not yet," Jim says. "I'm still getting things organized." In fact, Jim has done nothing.

In this example, fear of failure has caused Jim to procrastinate. Unfortunately, if he continues on this track, his failure will be ensured. Do you see any of your own behavior in this tale? Are you avoiding an important task because of fear that you're not up to the job?

In most cases the best way to handle fear is to confront it directly. If you fear that you lack the training or resources to successfully complete an assignment, say so, and get the help you need. If your fear stems from a lack of self-confidence—as in Jim's case—defuse that fear through planning. Think through all the things you will have to do to successfully complete the job. And then get on with it. Fear is a mental obstacle that activity will help dispel.

Not Knowing Where to Begin

Some jobs—particularly big jobs, new jobs, and jobs with no defined steps—tempt us to say, "I don't know where to begin." And this lack of clarity encourages procrastination. Consider how you would respond if your boss said, "I'd like you to write a book on time management for our company." Where would you begin? If you could not find a clear entry point to the assignment you might be tempted to procrastinate by working on something else.

There are usually two remedies for this type of situation:

- Jump in anywhere. After you're in the game, it's likely that you will find a productive way forward, and this will reduce any inclination to procrastinate.

- Break the job into its component parts, as described earlier. Then specify the tasks necessary to complete each part. Arrange those tasks in a logical sequence. Then begin with the first task in that sequence—and keep moving forward.

Try these remedies the next time you find yourself procrastinating. You'll be more productive and will feel better about your work after you stop delaying and begin doing things that must be done.

Overreaching

Some people—mostly dedicated people—make the mistake of over-loading their schedules. Perhaps you're one of them. They take on new responsibilities and *then* try to figure out how they'll get the work done. Consider this example:

> *Harvey is a hard worker and is highly motivated to do good work. He is also willing to do whatever is necessary to help his team accomplish its goals. When Marcy, the team leader, says, "Someone should develop a proposal for the next stage of our project," most people hunch down in their seats or start looking at their notebooks. "Can someone take this on?" Marcy asks again. Seeing that no one else will volunteer, Harvey steps up to the task—as he always does. His behavior is so predictable, in fact, that his teammates know that if they resist the urge to volunteer long enough, Harvey eventually will step forward to do the work. And when he gets the work done, it's always done well, because he is a dedicated perfectionist. The problem is that Harvey has trouble getting things done on time because he has overloaded himself with commitments.*

People like Harvey are terrific employees, but they have one problem: They don't know how to say no. They make more commitments than they can handle. Consequently, their schedules are hopelessly overloaded, and they end up working nights and weekends—and still never get caught up.

Are you like Harvey? If you are, you should understand that trying to do too much has a negative impact on all areas of your life. Your professional life will be blighted by tasks that stand between you and your primary responsibilities and goals. After all, how many of your commitments are linked to your critical goals? You also run the risk of burnout. Your personal life may also suffer, especially if you rob time from evenings and weekends—time you should be spending with friends and family. You can avoid overloading yourself if you do the following:

- Know your key responsibilities and goals. In this way, you can differentiate between them and the tasks that others would like you to assume. If a task is not one of your responsibilities or goals, don't volunteer to take it on. Instead, determine which individual has responsibility for it. If you still feel compelled to play a part, do so as a helper to that individual, and without assuming responsibility for the job, as in this replay of the earlier example:

"Can someone take this on?" Marcy asks again. Seeing that no one will volunteer, Harvey replies, "I don't have time to take it on, but I'd be willing to help if someone else will take responsibility for it."

- Resist the urge to step in and take over because others are not doing their jobs or not doing it to your standards. In many cases this is a delegation problem. If your subordinates are the ones making a mess of things, remember that they will never improve if you step in to do their work for them. Instead, provide some on-the-spot coaching or get them the help or training they need to do the work right.

- Don't assume that everything must be done. Not everything that people think of must be done. Remember the 80/20 rule: Twenty percent of actions will account for 80 percent of important outcomes. The other 80 percent simply don't have much impact. So concentrate on the 20 percent that matter, and stay away from the rest.

- Learn to say no to your peers and to your boss. Saying no is not easy if you have an accommodating personality or see yourself as a team player. But if you don't know how to say no, you'll end up like Harvey and never get your work done.

Saying no is a lot easier when you can articulate *why* you're doing it. The *why* of saying no becomes clear when you consider the consequence of saying yes—destroying your ability to get priority jobs done on time. The big challenge, of course, is learning to say no to your boss when saying yes is much easier. Saying yes to the boss will make you look good in the short term. In the Harvey example, Marcy will think, "I can always count on Harvey to do the jobs that no one else will do." But if always saying yes undermines your ability to handle priority jobs, you will end up looking like a loser. Nor will saying yes necessarily lead to a promotion; Marcy will think, "I need Harvey where he is now; I cannot get along without him." Bosses don't like to promote people whom they view as indispensable to their personal agendas.

Here's a strategy for coping when your boss asks you to take on added responsibilities that you simply cannot fit into your schedule:

1. Don't say anything definite before you've thought it through. Ask for a time-out. "Can we talk about it tomorrow afternoon?"

2. Use your time-out to prepare a response.

3. When you meet with your boss, list the projects you are currently working on and ask the boss to decide how these many projects—yours and the proposed one—should be prioritized. This will put the ball in the boss's court.

Here's an example:

John, a regional sales manager, was having lunch with his boss, Walter, the vice president of sales. "John, I'm worried about the inroads that low-carbohydrate snack foods are making into our sales," Walter said. "I'm seeing more and more of the Carbolite brand tortilla chips on shelves where our stuff ought to be."

"I know what you mean," John replied. "They seem to be everywhere this year."

"Tell you what," said the boss, "I'd like you to study it. Find out the amount of shelf space Carbolite's products are getting from stores, and then estimate their turnover relative to ours. You could ask our reps to gather the information."

"In my region?"

"No, for the entire country. And within the next few months."

John felt an uneasy sensation in his stomach. This was his boss talking. Walter was asking him to take on a task of national scope during the busiest time of year. On the one hand, John was flattered that his boss would entrust him with something so large and important. On the other hand, he had neither the resources nor the time to do it—unless Walter would shift some of John's regular responsibilities to someone else. Nor was market research one of his responsibilities.

John had to find a way to say no while remaining a team player. "Great idea," he told his boss. "If there's a trend toward low-carb snacks, we need to know about it. Would you mind if I gave that some thought between now and tomorrow afternoon?"

"Sure. Let's talk again tomorrow at two o'clock."

John used some of that time to develop a response to his boss's request. When they met, John said, "I agree that we must get a handle on the low-carb trend, and soon. But let me propose an alternative. We are just entering our busiest sales season, and I have three inexperienced sales reps to work with. You've given me a sales target of twenty million dollars for the year, and I am committed to it. But I won't hit that target if I divert my attention to this project at this critical time. So here's my suggestion: Let's revisit this project three months from today, after the busy season. In the meantime, I'll ask Sheila Evans in market research to develop a plan for capturing the data. How does that sound?"

Notice that John didn't say no in this example. Instead, he restated his assigned goal and his commitment to it. He then explained why the added work suggested by his boss would jeopardize that goal. Finally, John offered a reasonable alternative and asked his boss to decide on how he should spend his time.

The key point in this strategy is to affirm the priority of your critical goals and determine whether and to what extent taking on added work will interfere with progress toward those goals. If you do those two things, you will tame the problem of overreaching.

Of course, not every boss will be as reasonable and rational as John's. Any reluctance to do whatever the boss says could earn you a black mark in the boss's book. So know whom you are dealing with before trying this approach.

Assuming Subordinates' Problems

Some of the time squeeze experienced by managers may be self-imposed through a failure to delegate. Ideas on how you can become a better delegator are covered elsewhere in this book. But some individuals make themselves victims of reverse delegation: They allow subordinates to delegate problems to them, their managers. These managers end up taking on problems that their subordinates should be handling.

Do you find yourself spending an inordinate amount of time dealing with your subordinates' problems? If you do, you're not alone. This problem was addressed by William Oncken Jr. and Donald Wass in their classic *Harvard Business Review* article, "Management Time: Who's Got the Monkey?"[1] The authors ask, "Why is it that managers are typically running out of time while their subordinates are typically running out of work?" Their answer: Managers inadvertently take the monkey (that is, the problem) off the subordinate's back and place it on their own. Before long, they are weighted down with problems that their people should have handled—and they have little time left for their own work.

Subordinates are only too eager to shift their problems onto their boss's back. After all, doing so lightens their own load. And many inexperienced managers, in their eagerness to support their people, are easy marks. This is not to say that managers shouldn't help subordinates. It only means that they should help subordinates solve their own problems. Oncken and Wass have a hypothetical boss telling one of his people, "When this meeting is over, the problem will leave this office exactly the way it came in—on your back."

A subordinate, according to the authors, should be allowed to seek counsel from his or her manager on the problem, but only to report progress or problems in handling it. That's good advice. Follow it, and many of your time problems will go away.

Unnecessary Travel

Travel is often a necessary component of business. People must visit customers and suppliers face-to-face in order to establish personal relationships, and they must attend meetings or work on projects with fellow employees in other parts of the country or the world. In other cases, travel is a component of investigation and a spur to idea generation. Trade and scientific conferences are only two examples.

Roger is an acquisitions editor for a New York–based publishing company, and finance is one of the subject areas for which he is responsible. Every year he aims to find and contract fifteen books on the cutting edge of portfolio management, investment banking, securities analysis, and related areas. He develops many leads to potential authors by reading the Wall Street Journal, *the* Journal of Portfolio Management, Fortune, *academic journals, and a variety of business magazines. In addition, Roger spends time on the phone talking to literary agents, business professors, and money managers. He also travels to professional conferences to develop contacts and gain exposure to new practices in the world of finance and capital markets. "Every time I come back from one of those conferences," he tells a colleague, "I have three or four good ideas, and one of those eventually becomes a published book a year or two down the road."*

For Roger, travel is a must, not an obsession. Because of the cost in time and money, he travels only when he cannot achieve his ends by other means. He also prepares scrupulously for every trip by setting up many appointments, from breakfast through dinner. He packs the day to make the most of his travel.

Is your travel less productive than Roger's? Do you find yourself flying halfway across the continent to attend a three-hour meeting of dubious importance and then catching the next plane home? Do you have a real business purpose for attending meetings like this? Do these meetings measurably advance your goals, or do you attend because of a sense of obligation? Because travel consumes so much time, every businessperson should routinely assess its value, where value is defined as the benefits relative to costs.

The next time you take a business trip to attend a meeting or visit a branch office—or anything similar—keep track of the hours spent in valueless activities: getting to the airport, waiting around in the terminal, getting to your destination, taking a cab from the airport, returning home, and so forth. Then estimate what those hours have cost your company in terms of salary and benefits. Add that figure to the cost of transportation, lodging, and meals. Then make a mental comparison between the value produced by your trip and its financial cost. Is there a net benefit or a net loss?

Tips for Making the Most of Your Travel Time

If travel is essential, make the most of it. Here are a few tips:

- Take along enough paperwork to turn wasted time in terminals and taxis into productive time.

- If the purpose of your travel is a meeting, be totally prepared when you arrive. This will help ensure the effectiveness of the meeting and boost the value of your travel.

- Flying provides something that every manager needs desperately but cannot get in the office: interruption-free time. Use that quiet time to plan and think. Amazon's Jeff Bezos says, "I use flight time to catch up on the world, reading newspapers and magazines. I'll also sit with a notepad and brainstorm."[a]

- Make the very most of your travel days. If you must travel to San Francisco for a morning meeting, don't jump on the earliest flight home. Instead, make the most of the rest of your day in that city. For example, spend the afternoon with your company's local sales representative making calls. Or try to meet with an important customer or a strategic ally of the company. Even if you are a manufacturing manager or CFO, you'll learn a lot about customers and your competition by joining a front-line salesperson on regular calls.

[a] George Anders, "Bezos Shares His Ideas for Time Management," *Wall Street Journal*, February 4, 2000.

Then consider the opportunity cost of your trip: the value you could have produced if you had stayed in your office and done something else. If you hadn't taken that trip you could have done any number of value-adding activities:

- Coached a subordinate to improve her skills

- Taken an important customer to lunch and possibly gotten a new order

- Developed a more efficient work plan for your subordinates or team

- Used the telephone to speak with four or five potential customers

Some executives feel that travel is essential. This is surely true in many cases, but not all. Many of the benefits once created through travel can now be generated just as well—and at much lower cost—through travel alternatives, such as conference calls, Web conferences, and videoconferences. If you haven't already done so, investigate the potential of these travel alternatives. (You'll read more about this later in the book.)

E-mail and Paperwork

E-mail may be the most valuable new communication tool of the past few decades. With e-mail, you can send a text message, a scanned image, or an attached document to people on the next floor or on the other side of the globe. It's fast, convenient, and inexpensive. But because of the way people are using it, e-mail is becoming a major time robber. Consider the case of Paula, a project manager for a large manufacturing company.

Paula arrives at her desk at 8:45 a.m. every business day. Once her PC is up and running, her first act is to check her e-mail. "I have mixed feelings about it," she confesses. "On the one hand, I look forward to updates on company activities that concern me directly. And I also enjoy finding messages from friends. On the other hand, I dread facing the twenty or thirty e-mails that are either misdirected or irrelevant to me. And another twenty or thirty messages will hit my inbox before the day is over. Worse, I have to open most of them to find out that they are irrelevant."

Paula is not an exception. Executives, managers, and employees are bombarded with e-mail. According to a 2003 study by Ferris Research, people who variously work from home, the office, and travel several days each month receive forty to fifty nonspam messages every day, send twenty-five messages daily, and are hit by seventy spams per week. According to the research, independent consultants send and receive roughly the same number of messages but are on the receiving end of three hundred fifty spams weekly.[2]

Dealing with this volume of e-mail eats up plenty of time. Of course, not all that time is wasted because communication is an essential part of an organization's work. In fact, on balance, the productivity benefits of e-mail are high, easily outpacing its time-wasting costs. Those costs would be less, however, if we did not allow spam, personal messages, jokes, chain letters, and misdirected correspondence to clutter our in-boxes and distract us from our goals. Here are some tips for getting control of your e-mail before it takes control of you:

- Deal with e-mail at scheduled times during the day. Unless you are anxiously awaiting a message that will require your immediate attention, don't open every e-mail as it hits your in-box. Instead, check it at a few assigned times—for example, at 9:30 a.m., just after lunch, and again as the day winds down to closing time. This practice will reduce interruptions.

- Maintain a separate e-mail account for personal messages. Encourage nonbusiness correspondents to use that personal address exclusively. Check those messages when you are at home or on a lunch break.

- Use a systematic approach. You'll get through a long list of unopened mail if you follow this approach: First, delete all junk e-mail and the irrelevant messages that people feel compelled to copy to you. Do this quickly. Second, move all urgent messages to a special folder labeled "Urgent Mail"; deal with these at a specified time in your schedule. Finally, sweep any others that merit your eventual attention to a folder marked "Later." Deal with them only *after* you've addressed all the high-priority tasks on your schedule.

- Educate your correspondents. Let people know your information preferences and priorities. Send a reply stating, "Keep sending information on this," or "Please don't copy me on this information," or "Please direct future information on this subject to (name of appropriate subordinate)." Do this for a week or two, and fewer valueless messages will come your way.

Finally, the organization should encourage people to be explicit in filling in the subject line of their messages. The subject line should give the recipient a clear idea of the e-mail's message—enough that the recipient will know whether to delete the message, act on it immediately, or put it in the Later folder. Table 4-1 contains examples of effective and ineffective subject lines.

Don't Behave Like Pavlov's Dogs

Just as Ivan Pavlov used a bell to make dogs salivate in anticipation of a meal, incoming e-mail has trained many of us to put down what we are doing and go fetch it. Microsoft's ubiquitous Outlook Express rings a chime when a message arrives, tempting recipients to drop what they are doing, open the e-mail, and read the message. Most of us do the same when the telephone rings, even when we are doing something very important. This behavior creates discontinuity in the processes of work and thought, making us less efficient.

There are two ways to break the Pavlovian e-mail response. The first is to simply turn off the chime. In Outlook Express, go to Tools and then Options. Then open the General tab, and uncheck the box labeled "Play sound when new messages arrive." The second way is to go to the same General tab and adjust the checkbox that says "Check for messages every _____ minutes." Set the box to 90 minutes or some other appropriate interval. Doing this will significantly cut down the number of your interruptions.

TABLE 4-1

Effective and Ineffective Subject Lines

Effective	Ineffective
Sales meeting Tuesday at 2 p.m.	Meeting
Your market forecast needed by 3 p.m. today	Marketing project
How about lunch tomorrow?	(subject line left blank)
John's report attached FYI	Report

Effective subject lines contain sufficient information for the recipient to decide how to handle the message without opening it. The same cannot be said for ineffective subject lines. Each would have to be opened and read.

Although e-mail has taken the place of paper mail and memos to a large extent, most office workers continue to receive and respond to lots of paper. Employ this time-tested method for dealing with paperwork:

- If a paper communiqué doesn't require a response from you, skim it quickly and then toss or file it as appropriate.

- If a response is required and if doing so will take only a moment, respond then and there. Then toss or file the paper communiqué.

- If a response is required and you are too busy to deal with it at the moment, ask yourself, "Can I delegate this?" If you cannot delegate it, then immediately put the letter or memo into your Later folder, ranked by priority. For example, if you receive an invoice to be paid, you might place it directly into an invoice file for later payment. Block out a period of time in your weekly schedule to handle "Later" paperwork.

The idea is to dispose of paperwork quickly, in one way or another. This will help you avoid handling paper documents more than once.

Time–Wasting Meetings

If you're like most managers, you are spending 30–50 percent of your working hours in meetings. That's not too much time if your meetings are highly effective in accomplishing your goals, but it is too much time if they accomplish little.

Some people speculate that changes in the workplace have made meetings more necessary. These changes include employee empowerment (which makes coordination more necessary), a greater reliance on cross-functional teams, more consensus-based decision making, and increased numbers of alliances between companies. Whatever the reason for the many meetings we all experience, meetings are an essential part of organizational life.

For all the grousing we hear about them, however, the complaints are not about meetings per se but about those that devour time without producing tangible benefits. These wasteful meetings

- are unnecessary

- don't follow an agenda

- turn into gab sessions

- are dominated by one or two individuals who do all the talking

- run over schedule

- fail to produce decisions or commit people to action

- do not hold people accountable for their action assignments

Do the meetings you attend have any of these characteristics? If they do, it's no wonder that you think of them as time wasters. Contrast these with well-run meetings, in which people feel that they are sharing valuable information, participating in a key decision, or completing an important task. People don't complain about these meetings because important things are being accomplished; they may even lose track of the time.

Meeting-Free Days

Is your typical week fragmented by meetings, leaving you little time to complete assignments, travel, talk with suppliers, or simply schedule the next day's work? If it is, consider a department or company policy of meeting-free days.

Start small by putting Friday afternoons off-limits. If people express satisfaction with that regime—and if all the work gets done—consider expanding to an entire meeting-free day. Naturally, exceptions can be made to accommodate visiting customers and suppliers.

Some companies have a two-hour off-site meeting each quarter that involves the entire office work force. Because this and transportation time eat up most of the morning, a no-meeting afternoon may be in order on those days.

Warning: Meeting-free days work only if employees, including senior management, respect the policy. If people are allowed to encroach on meeting-free days, the policy will quickly become irrelevant.

Here are some things you can do to avoid time-wasting meetings:

- **Eliminate unnecessary meetings.** The purpose of a meeting is to facilitate interaction between attendees: to share opinions and ideas, to coordinate action, or to make a decision. Absent a need for these, you probably don't need a meeting.

- **Avoid meetings you have little to contribute to or little or nothing to gain from.** Just because someone has invited you to a meeting does not mean that you must attend (unless that person is your boss). This is doubly true if the inviter runs ineffective meetings.

- **Ask for an agenda before committing to a meeting.** If, after reviewing the agenda, you must ask "What's the point?" then avoid the meeting.

If you are organizing the meeting, make sure that "the point" is clear, important, and reflected in the agenda. Keep the meeting short and on topic, and don't allow it to run over schedule. Make sure that you've invited the right people—that is, people with an inherent interest in the subject, those who have important information, and those who have the authority to participate in a decision. Finally, be action-oriented. Your meeting should result in a decision, move people closer to a goal, or seek closure on an important matter. In the end, you want people to leave your meeting saying, "That took an hour, but we got that business behind us," or "Each of us now has an assignment."

Note: For more on this topic, see appendix C. This appendix also includes a handy checklist for planning your meetings.

Distractions and Switching Costs

Office settings are full of distractions. There's today's *Wall Street Journal* to read. E-mails from colleagues and friends. Conversations with coworkers around the coffee machine. And, of course, there's the Internet, which tempts us to check in periodically for the latest news headlines, the weather report, sport scores, movie reviews, and so forth. Each of these distractions stands between you and the things that need doing.

Distractions don't simply take you away from productive work; they actually set you back. This is because distractions shift your attention, creating switching costs every time you set down and pick up the same piece of work. Switching costs result when people must go back and review what they've done before they can resume work on a task. The more complicated the task, the longer it will take for you to become fully engaged, and the greater the cost. One study estimates that switching costs can reduce a company's efficiency by 20 to 40 percent.[3] This represents a huge and unrecognized drain on productivity. Consider this example:

> *Max has been working on a long, two-part report for the past two hours. He has managed to draft the first part and is ready to begin the second. Feeling that a little reward is in order, Max gets up and heads for the coffee room, where he refills his cup and chats briefly with two colleagues. Settling back into his desk a few minutes later, Max notices that he has two new e-mails. "I'd better check these out," he tells himself.*
>
> *After he replies to those messages, Max revisits his report. But he can't start where he left off—he has lost his train of thought. The only way to get it back is to reread what he's already written, a five-minute chore.*

Max's problem is commonplace in the typical office. E-mail, incoming phone calls, unscheduled visitors, and trips to the coffee room create distractions that interrupt our work and add extra time to the completion of tasks. There are several ways to avoid these distractions. Here are only a few:

- Have your voice-mail system pick up calls when you're busy.
- Turn off your e-mail.
- Clear your desk of newspapers and other distractions.
- If you have an office, close the door—and put a "Busy" sign on it.

Your aim, whenever feasible, should be to complete every task before you put it down. This parallels the long-standing time-management advice of never touching the same piece of paper twice.

A Useful Tool for Handling Time Robbers

Use a solution chart like the one shown in figure 4-1 to identify your time robbers, their cause, and possible solutions. After you have tried your solution, assess how well it worked. Simply going through this exercise will make you more aware of things that steal your time.

FIGURE 4-1

Time Robbers Solutions Chart

Time Robber	Cause	Solution	How Well Your Solution Worked		
			Not Effective	Effective	Very Effective
E-mail	Friends and family send jokes and messages	Handle nonbusiness messages during lunch break only		X	
" "	" "	Request people not to bother me at work.	X		
Inefficient meetings	No focus or poor agenda control	Insist on more focus or find reasons not to attend.		X	
		Avoid pointless meetings.			X
Office distractions	Boring or difficult tasks	Resolve to complete tasks before dealing with e-mail and phone calls.		X	

Source: Adapted from Harvard ManageMentor® on Time Management, adapted with permission.

You will never get rid of all distractions, but there is one simple and helpful device for vanquishing most of them—one that sales-people and managers have used for a long time with good results. Simply attach a note with the following message to your telephone console, your desk, your computer monitor, or somewhere else where you cannot avoid seeing it:

> Is What I'm Doing
> Right Now
> Moving Me Toward
> My Goal?

If you become distracted, that little message can often shift your focus back to the things that matter.

Another way to reduce switching costs is to concentrate on a single task until it is finished. When that task is complete, move on to the next one.

Summing Up

- Procrastination has three causes: The task is unpleasant or uninteresting, you are afraid you will fail, or you do not know where to begin.

- Don't take on new responsibilities without first figuring out whether you have time to complete them.

- You can avoid overloading your schedule by consciously recognizing your key goals, delegating to others, observing the 80/20 rule (that 20 percent of your actions will account for 80 percent of important outcomes), and learning to say no when others try to pile more work onto your back.

- Avoid assuming the responsibilities and problems of your subordinates. Coach them and advise them, but don't allow them to put the monkey on your back.

- Avoid needless travel. When you must travel, take along work you can do to fill idle hours, and fill as many hours of your trip as possible with productive activities.

- Get control of your e-mail by dealing with it at scheduled times during the day, using your business e-mail address for business purposes only, and deleting unwanted messages without opening them.

- Deal with paperwork in a manner that prevents you from handling the same piece of paper more than once.

- Meetings can be major time wasters. Do your best to eliminate meetings that are not necessary, and avoid meetings you have little to contribute to or little to gain from. Also avoid meetings that lack a clear agenda.

- Diverting your attention from one activity to another, and back again, produces switching costs that deplete your time. There are two remedies for the problem of switching costs: Avoid distractions, and concentrate on a single task until it is finished before moving to the next.

5

Delegation

Gaining Time for Yourself

Key Topics Covered in This Chapter

- *Signs that you should do more delegating or more effective delegating*

- *Guidelines for effective delegating*

- *Approaches to delegation*

- *Preparing to delegate*

- *Making the assignment*

- *Monitoring performance*

- *Learning through after-action review*

DELEGATION IS THE assignment of a specific task or project by one person to another, and the assignee's commitment to complete the task or project. When you delegate, you not only transfer work to another person but also transfer accountability for completing that work to stated standards.

Delegation is one of the most important skills demonstrated by successful managers, and one often neglected by supposedly "overworked" managers who cannot find enough hours in the day to complete their work. Effective delegators spend less time "doing" and more time planning work assignments, organizing resources for others, and coaching people who need help. In contrast, managers who fail to delegate effectively always find themselves out of time and buried under work they cannot complete. This chapter explains the timeless principles of delegating and offers practical ideas for applying them today.[1]

The Benefits of Delegating

Effective delegation can have real benefits for you, your people, and your organization. Let's start with you. When you delegate, you reduce your workload and stress level by removing tasks from your to-do list that others are qualified to handle. If you do this, you will discover that you have more time to focus on tasks that require your unique skills and authority: planning, conducting business analysis, controlling operations, obtaining resources, dealing with people problems, and just plain thinking about how to improve the business.

Delegating is also a good way to build a solid understanding of subordinates and their individual capabilities. If you assign a series of tasks and observe how the employee performs, you'll soon have a good understanding of that person's strengths and weaknesses. That type of understanding will help you know who is ready for a promotion, who needs skill training, and where you can apply effective coaching.

Delegating also improves the level of trust between you and your subordinates. To get trust, you must first give trust, and delegating is one of the best ways to do it. The message in delegation is, "I trust you to get this job done."

Good employees benefit from delegation. Every assignment is an opportunity for them to accept responsibility, to plan work, and to enlist the collaboration of others. In effect, delegating gives employees experience with managerial work. And developing subordinates, if you are a manager, is an important part of your job.

Finally, the organization benefits from delegation, particularly when subordinates are empowered with some level of decision-making authority. Because subordinates are often closer to customers and to the daily workings of the business than their managers, they are in a good position to make decisions that will benefit the company.

Some managers are uneasy about delegation because they fear losing control. Others worry that they're abdicating their responsibilities. Still others believe that it's more efficient to do the job themselves: "In the time it takes for me to explain the job to Henry, I could do it myself." And maybe they can. In the long term, however, every manager must share some control and teach others how to do the work. Other excuses for insufficient delegating include the following:

"I don't have confidence in my staff." These managers should start delegating small tasks; this will allow them to build confidence gradually.

"I like to have things done my way." This should not be an impediment. Managers can get things done their way by communicating preferences and standards. That's more efficient than trying to do everything by themselves.

"My staff will resent the additional work." Maybe so. But good employees—the ones you want to keep—appreciate opportunities to take responsibility for important work.

"People expect me to be the problem solver and decision maker." That's true to an extent, but problem solvers and decision makers are needed at all levels. Make it clear that your role is to support your staffers in making certain decisions for themselves. Also, make it clear that some delegated tasks represent opportunities to do new and interesting work.

Warning Signs

Here are some warning signs that a manager's delegating skills require sharpening. Do any apply to you?

- Your in-box is always full.

- You are regularly working overtime on tasks that "only you can do."

- Delegated assignments are often incomplete, and deadlines are missed.

- Direct reports feel that they lack the authority or resources to complete assignments.

- You second-guess your subordinates' decisions and personally rework their assignments.

- Direct reports feel unprepared to carry out assigned tasks.

- You frequently intervene in projects assigned to others.

- Morale is low and staff turnover is rising.

- People are not taking responsibility for the tasks you delegate.

Guidelines for Effective Delegating

It is crucial to establish the right tone and environment for effective delegating. You can do this if you follow these guidelines:

- Be very clear about what you want done, and about when and how results will be measured. Ambiguity will lead only to a disappointing experience.

- Encourage subordinates to tell you about their special interests at work and about the time they have available for new projects.

- Build a sense of shared responsibility for the unit's overall goals. Those goals shouldn't be your goals alone.

- Avoid dumping only tedious or difficult jobs on your subordinates. Instead, delegate tasks that spark interest and can be enjoyable.

- Provide career opportunities for others by delegating functions that have high visibility within the company.

- Delegate to people whose judgment and competence you trust. This, of course, requires that you know your subordinates and their capabilities very well.

- Recognize that delegation is a learning experience for your staff, so offer training or coaching as needed.

- Develop trust in less-skilled staff members by delegating highly structured assignments. Then provide the support they need to increase their competence.

- Whenever possible, delegate an entire project or function and not just a small piece; doing this will increase motivation and commitment.

- Monitor progress and provide feedback.

- Maintain open lines of communication. Say, "Let me know if you run into problems."

Approaches to Delegation

Delegation can be carried out in several ways. It is usually best to delegate responsibility for an entire task, project, or function to one person. Dividing it among several people will create a condition in which no one "owns" the job. And if no one owns it, it will not be done well.

Delegating by task is the easiest approach and a good place to start if you're new to this. It involves assigning a specific task: writing a report, doing research, or planning a meeting.

Delegating by project represents a higher level of delegation. It increases the scope of the delegation assignment and generally requires a delegatee who can handle a wide range of responsibilities. Examples of project delegation might include developing a new employee handbook, conducting a customer survey, or training other employees on a new piece of computer software.

Managers with many direct reports may choose to delegate assignments by function. A function refers to groups of tasks and projects that are all related to one ongoing activity, such as sales, marketing, or training. In this approach, each function is delegated to one staff member, who provides the manager with regular updates on activities within that function.

Preparing to Delegate

As you prepare to delegate, first determine which tasks you want to delegate. Then consider the skills and capabilities required to complete the assignment successfully. Finally, match the assignment with the most appropriate staff member.

What (and What Not) to Delegate

Is your workload crushing you? If it is, assess it. Determine which parts of it others can handle. Be open to delegating these, even if they are jobs you enjoy doing and don't want to give up. Some of those chores could provide variety and motivational challenges to the right individuals.

Some assignable jobs require specific training or experience. And if a task is too important to assign to others, think about sharing the responsibility—while assigning dual ownership. For example, if you have a brochure development project, identify one person with excellent writing skills to write the text; team this person with someone who has graphics, layout, and production skills.

Here's another example:

One of Colin's responsibilities during the first half of this year was to design, administer, and document an annual employee survey. This was a big job, but not so big that Colin couldn't handle it himself—as he had in previous years.

But times had changed. Now that he was the department manager, Colin had very little time to spare. Yes, he could still do this job himself, but that would involve many weekends in the office and would take time away from other pressing responsibilities.

In the end, Colin formed a task force to handle the survey. He provided leadership and oversight, and two new employees with good analytical skills were assigned the time-consuming parts of the job. When the final survey report was circulated within the company, it bore the names of Colin and his two helpers.

Of course, not all tasks can or should be delegated. As a manager, you should retain responsibility for such things as

- planning, directing, and motivating your people

- employee performance evaluation

- complex customer negotiations

- tasks requiring your specific technical skills

- hiring, firing, and career development.

Other nonassignable tasks will depend on your circumstances

Task Analysis

After you've identified tasks or projects that are suitable for delegation, determine the work involved and skills required. Task analysis
involves answering these three questions:

- What thinking skills are needed for this job? Examples might
  include problem-solving ability, logical thinking, decision making, planning, and creative design.

- What activities must be performed, and what equipment is
  needed? Examples are filing, using a word processor, organizing, training, and developing.

- What interpersonal skills are needed to complete the assignment? Examples include speaking with suppliers, negotiating
  for resources, and consulting with experts.

The Right Person for the Job

After you have identified the assignment and the required skills, ask
yourself, "Which of my subordinates is the right person for the
job?" As you ponder this question, be sure to consider the following:

- Any previously expressed desire by staffers for growth and development that could be addressed with this assignment. Ask
  yourself who has shown initiative and asked for a new challenge. But remember that it is the boss's job to figure out what
  people's development needs are. It is not simply the subordinates' expressed desire for development opportunities but the
  boss's accurate assessment of them that should drive delegation
  decisions.

- The staff member's availability. Don't pile work onto people
  who are already loaded to the limit—even if they are conscien-
  tious and reliable.

- The level of assistance a staff member will need from you to
  complete the assignment.

- How long the staff member has been on the job. Avoid loading new employees with added assignments until they are comfortable with their core jobs.

- The number of previous assignments you have delegated to that person. Try to delegate tasks among all staff members to avoid any feelings of favoritism.

- The possibility of dividing the task between two or more people to make the best use of skills.

You'll be in a better position to select the right people if you routinely keep track of special skill sets that you may need to call upon for special projects. For example, someone who can simplify abstract concepts might make a good trainer, whereas good organizational abilities would be important for someone overseeing operations.

Making the Assignment

After you've matched the right person with the task, you need to communicate the proposition and deliver sufficient authority to do the job. This should always be done in a face-to-face meeting in which you describe the assignment and secure the employee's acceptance of the task. Open communication and trust are critical factors in this interaction. To achieve both, do the following:

- Clearly describe the task, project, or function.

- Define its purpose and explain how it fits into the big picture.

- Review the scope of the employee's responsibilities.

- Identify other personnel who will be involved, if applicable, and describe their roles.

- Discuss feasible deadlines for completion.

- Establish standards of performance, measures of success, and levels of accountability.

- Set firm metrics for such things as quality, time, and cost.

- Be clear about the employee's accountability in meeting the standards you have agreed upon.

- Define the resources and support that will be available.

- Identify any materials and physical resources needed to complete the assignment, and confirm their availability.

- If necessary, allocate additional staff to assist in meeting the assigned goals.

- Ask the employee what support she thinks she may need from you throughout the assignment.

- If special training or coaching is needed, discuss how it will be given.

- Agree on a date to review progress.

Delegation to a subordinate often involves the granting of some authority. In granting authority, it is important to establish clear guidelines and expectations from the start. The amount of authority you choose to give an individual depends upon his capabilities and your confidence in him. You will want to assess the staff member's past performance as a decision maker. You'll also want to determine the minimum amount of authority needed to complete the assignment successfully.

After you have determined the level of authority you will delegate, be sure to communicate your decision to everyone involved in the assignment or affected by it.

Control, Monitoring, and Feedback

The biggest challenge for the delegating manager is to ensure that the subordinate does not fail. The best way to do that is to maintain an adequate level of control by providing target completion dates and regular monitoring of progress. When you say, "I want this done by next Friday," you are maintaining control of the work, and that is your duty as manager. When you add, "I'd like to meet with you on Wednesday afternoon, just to see how you're progressing and to discuss any problems," you are monitoring the delegated assignment. Monitoring provides opportunities to give coaching and feedback, another key responsibility of every manager.

Depending on the number and complexity of assignments you've delegated, you can use an assignment log to track all projects, tasks, or functions within your department. Other managers use large wall calendars to keep track of delegated assignments and to give a visual sense of progress. Still others require periodic written status reports to keep up-to-date on the assignments they have delegated.

In monitoring, be alert to early signs of trouble. When your subordinate hits a barrier or begins to fall behind, intervention may be necessary. Of course, you don't want to solve every problem that you've delegated to others—and that they have accepted. Doing so would defeat your purpose. So use coaching, encouragement, and added resources as you see fit to help them help themselves. Provide this support without being intrusive, especially when subordinates are committed to learning how to handle things by themselves, and without

Tips for Delegating Effectively

- Recognize the capabilities of your staff.

- Focus on results. Let go of any urge to dictate how tasks should be accomplished.

- Use delegation to develop the skills of your staff or to position people favorably with senior management.

- Delegate to the lowest possible level.

- Explain assignments clearly, and provide the resources needed for successful completion.

- Provide feedback to your staff and support them through their mistakes.

dictating the "right way." Remember that accomplishing the task is more important than your idea of *how* it should be accomplished.

After–Action Review

Use completed assignments as opportunities for learning—for both you and your subordinate. When a job is completed, the two of you should evaluate what went right, what went wrong, and how things might have been done differently or better. In addition,

- ask for the employee's opinion about how this delegation worked for him

- recognize the employee's achievements and provide positive re-inforcement for tasks done well

- use the experience to support the employee's growth through ongoing coaching or additional training as needed.

You should also ensure that your employee is recognized for her good work, not only by you but also by peers, your manager, and customers, as appropriate.

Delegating is probably the most effective tool of time management available to executives, managers, and supervisors. Done well, it can clear your calendar of jobs that others can and should be handling. You can use that extra time to tackle tasks having greater potential impact. Those high-impact tasks will take you beyond efficiency to something much more valuable: effectiveness.

Summing Up

- If you are overwhelmed with work and your subordinates are not, you need to do more delegating. If the tasks you delegate are done poorly or late, you need to become a more effective delegator.

The U.S. Army on After-Action Review

The U.S. Army has institutionalized the process of after-action review (AAR) at both small- and large-group levels. It has even established a Center for Army Lessons Learned, where observers and facilitators are trained and where field-based learning is disseminated. As described by Harvard professor David Garvin, AAR is conducted immediately following an action and revolves around four questions:

- What did we set out to do?

- What actually happened?

- Why did it happen?

- What are we going to do next time?

Army doctrine recommends that 25 percent of the time spent on AAR be focused on the first two questions, 25 percent on the third question, and half the time on "What are we going to do next time?"

SOURCE: David A. Garvin, *Learning in Action* (Boston: Harvard Business School Press, 2000), 106–107.

- Effective delegators have several things in common. They are clear about what they want done; they delegate both tedious and stimulating tasks; and they monitor progress.

- It is usually best to delegate responsibility for an entire job to one person. That invests ownership of the job in a single person.

- Don't delegate tasks that are clearly your responsibility. That's abdication.

- Use a face-to-face meeting when you delegate, and always give sufficient authority and resources to get the job done.

- Monitor and be ready to intervene if the delegatee gets offtrack.

- Use after-action reviews to learn from the delegating experience.

6

The Time–Wasting Boss

How to Cope

Key Topics Covered in This Chapter

- *Clearing up time-wasting confusion about subordinate goals*

- *Dealing with a boss who fails to give clear directions*

- *Putting the brakes on the boss's pointless meetings*

- *What do to when the boss becomes a bottleneck*

EVERY EXECUTIVE, MANAGER, and supervisor is responsible for ensuring that subordinates are operating efficiently and effectively and working toward their assigned goals. This is a primary responsibility of management—getting results through people. Unfortunately, many bosses unknowingly create time-wasting impediments for their subordinates. They do this when they and their subordinates fail to reach an understanding about goals, when they fail to give clear directions, and when they involve subordinates in fruitless or unnecessary meetings.

Is your boss limiting your productivity or effectiveness with any of these impediments? This chapter examines these problems and suggests what you can do to prevent them from wasting your time. But there are two sides to this coin. Some people unwittingly behave in ways that waste their boss's time. We'll give you some tips for avoiding this problem.

Confusion About Goals

As emphasized earlier in this book, goals are the point of departure for all effective time management. Lacking clear goals, we have no basis for evaluating our time-spending patterns or prioritizing our tasks, and no sense of what is important and what isn't. If goals are not clear or understood, time management itself is a waste of time.

Consider, then, the case of a boss and a subordinate who haven't taken the time to talk about or agree on goals. They haven't specified goals in writing, haven't connected them to time frames, and haven't made them measurable and challenging or ensured their alignment with organizational strategy. The subordinate who lacks these things has no aiming point and no way of forming a coherent and prioritized set of tasks. And the boss has no sound basis for evaluating the subordinate's progress or performance. Consider this time-wasting example, as described by a marketing manager:

> Our CEO issued an edict on cost control, which my boss blithely passed on to us with an urgent deadline. We were told to cut costs. Unfortunately, this cost control edict had no criteria. Were we supposed to cut some percentage of individual spending? Was the CEO looking for some percentage of reduced spending within every operating unit? Or was he looking for a particular number, such as $2 million in total cuts? We had no idea, and he wasn't saying. The result was a frenzy of activity that was a big drain on our time and produced a poor outcome.

In this case, time was wasted because someone at the top hadn't taken the time to articulate the details of the goal. Strangely, some bosses never get around to this essential element of management: setting goals. If yours is one of them, take the initiative:

- Ask for a meeting to discuss your goals.

- During the meeting, collaborate on setting your goals for the coming year and for the next six months.

- Make sure that goals are specific, measurable, and so forth, as described earlier.

- Make sure that the goals are viewed as important and that they are aligned with your company's (or unit's) strategy.

- Watch out for misalignment between your goals and your company's rewards system. Be sure that you will be rewarded—and not penalized—as you work toward and achieve your assigned goals.

- Give some thought to your ability to accomplish the assigned goals. Do you have the necessary skills and resources? If you don't, talk with your boss about additional training or resources.

Once the two of you are in agreement, get those goals in writing, and make sure that the document goes into your personnel file. Meet again with your boss at regular intervals to discuss your progress and find out whether your goals are still relevant. Remember that changes in the environment can render goals irrelevant.

Failure to Give Clear Directions

Bosses who give inadequate directions or specifications for the work they want done appear to be near the top of the list of time wasters, according to a number of managers and professionals interviewed for this chapter. Here is one testimonial. Does it sound familiar?

> *I was one of three product managers reporting to Stan, a very ineffective boss. Responding to a demand from his own boss, Stan called us all to his office for a hastily planned meeting. "Listen," he said, "I want each of you to drop what you're doing and write me a report on the new products you have in the development pipeline, and how much revenue you expect them to produce in this fiscal year and the next." Stan wanted those reports by 3:00 p.m. the next day.*
>
> *So each of us went back to our respective offices, put aside everything else, and went to work on those reports. I must have spent seven or eight hours on mine, and my colleagues probably did the same. That's twenty-one to twenty-four total hours. And we gave Stan what he asked for. Two days later, Stan called us all back to his office, this time to tell us that we hadn't done the reports the way he wanted. He had a special format in mind, he wanted the revenues of current products integrated into the report, and on and on—all things he hadn't bothered to tell us during our previous meeting. So we had to go back and start over. If he had been clearer in the beginning about what he wanted, the three of us wouldn't have wasted all that time.*

Here's another true story, this one contributed from a manager in a financial services company:

> *We have a vice president whose biggest concern in life seems to be perfect PowerPoint slides. Whenever he has to make a presentation to se-*

nior management or the board, we have to drop everything and spend hours and hours on his slides. These go through many, many iterations before he accepts them because he never tells us what he wants. This VP must see something before he can decide that it meets his needs. So we'll take him a set of slides, and he'll look at them and say, "Can you make the fonts larger and change the background color?" He continues to demand changes until the presentation has been made.

Any big internal presentation—a strategic plan, budget, or project review—that he has to put forward for his own boss causes waves of anxiety among his direct reports, and that anxiety trickles down to the layers under us. We're all tied up in knots whenever this VP makes a presentation.

Naturally, this activity pulls resources away from attention we would otherwise give to our customers and to managing our own pieces of the business. If he would simply think through his requests before issuing them to us, we could do the job in less than half the time.

There are good reasons for senior managers to articulate a goal without spelling out the details of how they want the work done. One is to avoid micromanaging—to give subordinates opportunities to create their own solutions. In many scientific and engineering endeavors, for example, employees must solve complex problems for which there are no clear guidelines. In these cases, management must look to its talented and creative employees to find optimal solutions. The manager says, for example, "We need to design a military vehicle that is fuel efficient (25 miles per gallon on paved roads), that is capable of driving over rough terrain, and that can protect the driver and five passengers from small arms fire." Employees are told what the result should look like and are given responsibility for producing it.

This "results-mode" approach to management saves time for time-strapped bosses. Instead of specifying what people in different jobs should do and how they should do it, these managers can concentrate on providing the resources, training, and motivation that people need to produce the desired results.

During his tenure as CEO of Hewlett-Packard, John Young practiced this results-mode type of management. Every few years he would articulate a demanding, important, and clear goal and leave it to the company's talented personnel to find ways of achieving it. One year, for example, he called for a 90 percent reduction in the number of HP product failures, and he asked for that level of reliability within two years. In another case, he challenged company product developers to cut in half the time required to bring a new product idea to the point of product launch. In both instances, HP personnel successfully rose to the challenge—and without micromanagement by their CEO. Young would articulate a goal and leave it to employees to find their own ways to it.

But not every boss is a John Young. Some bosses want things done a certain way—and perhaps with good reason. But these managers then have an obligation to specify what they want and how they want it handled. Better still, they should communicate both the specifics of the job and the spirit or intent of their directives. Otherwise they risk reducing their own performance by wasting the valuable time of their people.

If your boss has a habit of not giving directions and then second-guessing your approach to the work, don't expect the problem to go away on its own. Your boss has developed a habit that will not go away without a gentle push. Here is a suggestion: When you get your orders, draft a preliminary plan for approaching the task. Then meet with your boss and say, "This is how I plan to approach this. What do you think?" Incorporate the boss's comments and criticisms into a revised plan, and get him to say, "Yes, that's the best way to handle this." If you do this often enough, your boss will realize that he can save time for himself by simply being specific the first time he explains the job. He will develop a new and better habit for dealing with you.

Pointless Meetings

Every white-collar worker has a litany of pointless meetings. Scott Adams, creator of the "Dilbert" cartoon series, has made a fortune by rendering meeting-from-hell stories sent to him by white-collar workers. Here are two pointless-meeting stories passed on by managers and executives. The first is from the CEO of a design firm:

> *My favorite pointless-meeting story involves a boss I had early in my career. He required every one of us to attend a daily staff meeting in which he would open the department's mail, read each letter aloud, and then ask us what we thought should be done in response to each item. This often took the entire morning.*

Another individual made this contribution:

> *We had a CEO who routinely took phone calls—often from his wife—during the course of meetings held in his office. The rest of us would have to sit there like a bunch of dummies until he finished. One episode in particular sticks in my mind. The CEO, me, the chief financial officer, and three others were discussing a project that would require a substantial capital investment. With the exception of me, this little group contained the highest-paid people in the company. Fifteen minutes into our deliberations, the CEO took a call from his wife that lasted at least twenty minutes. To keep my blood pressure from rocketing into the danger zone, I made a mental calculation of what each wasted minute was costing the company in salaries and benefits for the six of us. It was a large number. By the time the CEO said goodbye to his spouse, we didn't have enough time left to finish our discussion. We had to schedule another meeting to cover the same ground.*
>
> *After that episode, I always took along other work to the CEO's meetings. That work helped to fill the time while our brilliant leader was gabbing on the phone as if we and our issues didn't matter.*

Perhaps the worst type of wasteful meeting is the one in which the boss has already determined the desired outcome but forces her direct reports to go through the motions of reaching consensus. Some call this "faux collaboration." Consider this example, submitted by a middle manager:

> *Greg, our boss, holds a staff meeting every Thursday morning from 9 to 11. Everyone is encouraged to contribute ideas during these meetings, which, on the surface, makes it seem that we are shaping the outcome.*

But it's really a sham since Greg has already reached his conclusion. His suggestions always carry the day. These meetings are just his way of trying to make us believe that our ideas matter—which they don't. It's okay if he wants to make all the decisions; he's the boss. I just wish that he wouldn't waste our time with this weekly charade. Everyone else feels the same.

Greg's weekly staff meetings are truly pointless and annoying to everyone who is forced to participate in his charade. Meetings organized by your boss should set an example of effectiveness. Like every good meeting, they should be well organized, follow compact agendas, include all the right people, and lead to a decision or to action assignments. The people who attend meetings should feel that their time is being well spent and that they are contributing and benefiting in equal measure.

If your boss's meetings don't fit this description, do whatever you can to change the situation. For example, before the meeting begins in earnest, ask to make alterations to the agenda; find a subtle way of letting him know that you are impatient with the way those meetings are being handled.

The Bottleneck Boss

"I have a boss who wants everything to come through her," complained one midlevel manager. "Whether it's a change request or something as simple as an outgoing letter, she feels the need to see and approve it. The trouble is that she doesn't have the time to respond in a timely fashion. Consequently, most initiatives must wait and wait to proceed."

This person has just described a bottleneck boss. A *bottleneck boss* acts as a pinch-point in the work flow, causing work to back up. This wastes time for employees who must wait to complete their tasks.

A bottleneck condition may be unavoidable when oversight by a licensed professional is required by law, or when employee skills are untested or not to be trusted. These situations, however, are rare. In most others, the boss is simply a stickler for control. Here are a few ways to open the bottleneck:

- Do your homework. Assess the productivity losses caused by the bottleneck.

- Meet with your boss to discuss your findings and to seek remedies.

- Find remedies that your boss can live with. For example, identify tasks that can proceed without passing through the bottleneck; or urge the boss to delegate approval authority to you or someone else for less critical tasks.

The important thing here is to communicate the problem. The boss has an even greater interest than you do in promoting efficiency. She may deal with the problem once she is aware of it. If she will not address the problem, consider a job change. A bottleneck boss who will not change is an impediment to your career growth.

Your Role in the Problem

It is easy to poke fun at the shortcomings of our bosses and to complain about how they sometimes waste our time. It is far more difficult to see how our own modes of behavior waste the time of our superiors. Remember, your boss is as time constrained as you are, so take a look in the mirror and try to see how you might be a source of wasted time.

Avoid Unnecessary Requests

Are you requesting your boss's intervention too often, when you or one of your subordinates could accomplish the same thing without his help? In their classic article "Managing Your Boss," John Gabarro and John Kotter remark that every request you make of your boss uses up some of his resources; those requests also use up some of your limited capital with the boss. So don't make trivial or nonessential requests. Gabarro and Kotter cite the example of someone who failed to heed this advice:

> *One vice president went to great lengths to get his boss to fire a meddlesome secretary in another department. His boss had to use considerable influence to do it. Understandably, the head of the other department was not pleased. Later, when the vice president wanted to tackle more important problems, he ran into trouble. By using up his chips on a relatively trivial issue, he had made it difficult for him and his boss to meet more important goals.*[1]

Don't Delegate Problems to Your Boss

If you have subordinates of your own, the last thing you should allow them to do is delegate their problems to you. If you did, they would be in your office every fifteen minutes saying, "I can't figure out how to do this. Can you take care of it for me?" Ineffective managers make subordinates' problems their problems. Those managers eventually realize that their calendar is getting overloaded while their subordinates don't have enough work to fill the day.

Helping subordinates is part of a manager's job. The effective manager offers suggestions or the resources that subordinates need to solve their problems. But this manager makes sure that they leave the same way they came in—with the burden still on their backs.

Now examine your own behavior. Do you delegate upward, putting your problems on your boss's back? If you do, you are wasting that person's time.

Accommodate Your Boss's Work Style

Another way to avoid wasting your boss's time is to understand and accommodate her work style. Some executives insist on getting lots of information and detailed analysis from their subordinates; they are uncomfortable making a decision when more than 10 percent of the information isn't available. That is their style. Others trust more in their experience and intuition, making decisions with a minimum of data. Some executives are readers, whereas others are listeners.

Do you understand how your boss operates? Does she really want that mountain of spreadsheets and analyses you've just piled onto her desk, or would she prefer that you summarize the issues and options in a brief conversation? By understanding how your boss processes information, handles meetings, and makes decisions, you can help save lots of time for both of you.

You and your boss need each other. Mutual dependence makes it imperative that you build a strong relationship and learn to work together effectively. So take note of how your boss wastes your time and follow the advice in this chapter to improve the situation. Then take a sharp-eyed look at yourself, and try to recognize ways that you could become a more effective collaborator with people above and below you in the chain of command.

Summing Up

- Bosses unknowingly create time-wasting impediments when they and their subordinates fail to reach an understanding about goals, when bosses fail to give clear directions, when they involve subordinates in fruitless or unnecessary meetings, and when they create bottlenecks to forward progress.

- If your boss has not clearly stated your personal goals, ask for a meeting to reach agreement on your goals. Make those goals specific and measurable, and get it all in writing.

- The failure to give clear direction to subordinates is a major source of wasted time.

- Substantial time is wasted in pointless meetings. Bosses should set the standard for effective meetings. Their meetings should be well organized, follow compact agendas, include all the right people, and lead to a decision or to action assignments.

- A bottleneck boss creates a pinch-point in the work flow, causing work to back up. This wastes time for employees, who must wait to complete their tasks.

The Personal Side of Time

Mastering Work–Life Balance

Key Topics Covered in This Chapter

- *Goals as the starting point of personal time management*

- *Scheduling high-priority personal goals*

- *Making more room in your schedule by decluttering your life*

- *Dealing with personal commitments*

- *The role of fitness and health in personal time management*

- *Balancing your work and personal lives*

I T 'S TEMPTING TO think of your home as a refuge from the workplace. Picture the corporate warrior, numb and exhausted, walking through the front door of his home at the end of a long day. He tosses his briefcase in the corner, hangs up his coat, and pours a glass of wine before dropping onto the sofa. Ah! Isn't this more like it? The problem of having too much to do and too little time has temporarily been put on the shelf. Or has it?

Unfortunately, home isn't always a peaceful oasis. Especially for two-worker households with children, there is much to do and very limited time in which to do it. Children and personal relationships must be tended and nurtured. A sense of civic responsibility urges us to serve on school boards and to participate in town government and neighborhood associations. Our personal interests in music, literature, sports, and nature beg for attention. And then there's that leaky faucet that needs fixing.

In the United States, time shortage on the home front has been made worse by the uniquely American practice of expanding the number of hours we must be at work—or working on office projects at home. In her book *The Overworked American*, economist Juliet Schor documents how the typical American has been asked to work increasing numbers of hours. By her count, the average U.S. work year has grown nine hours per year over the past several decades.[1] An extra nine hours each year may not sound like much, but they add up over the years and cut directly into the time people would normally have available for family and personal matters.

Ironic, isn't it? People in the world's wealthiest nation are among the most impoverished in personal time. The more productive and prosperous Americans become, the more they are asked to work. By the late 1990s, the average American manufacturing employee was putting in three hundred twenty more hours each year than his or her counterpart in Europe. Whereas the typical European starting employee receives a month-long paid vacation, the newly hired American is lucky to get ten days.

Schor's research was completed in the late 1990s, just as laptops and e-mail were making major inroads into our lives. So you can add to her calculation the many hours that people now spend working at home and answering e-mails at night, on weekends, and during their vacations. These communications advances have turned many homes into satellite offices, where personal time is used to do work for which there were too few hours in the regular workplace.

You already know that you must gain control of your time at work. But that may not be possible if you don't do the same with the time you spend away from work—and vice versa. You need to get control of both sides of your life. This chapter applies concepts of time management to the home front and offers ideas for making the personal side of your life more effective and fulfilling.

Identify and Prioritize Your Personal Goals

Earlier chapters of this book provided a practical time-management methodology for your work life. They urged you to follow these steps:

1. Articulate critical and enabling goals.

2. Prioritize those goals and break them into tasks.

3. Use a daily log to understand how you currently spend your time and the extent to which unimportant activity crowds out the things that really matter to you.

4. Schedule priority tasks, leaving enough time open for unanticipated situations and opportunities.

This methodology is neither complex nor difficult, nor should it be made so. All that's required is the will to do it, and that usually springs from this simple recognition: "I have a problem. I'm not controlling my time; it's controlling me."

You can use this same methodology to gain control of the personal side of your life. As with your life at work, start with goals. What are your highest personal goals? Chances are that it will take you more time to answer that question than to answer the same question about your workplace goals. That's because workplace goals are hammered into our minds during performance reviews or whenever we look at our official job descriptions. This doesn't happen on the personal side of your life, which has many more dimensions to consider; and there are other important people in your life whose goals and preferences must be accommodated. There is no job description for being a successful parent, spouse, or friend. There is no boss to remind you, "This year, you should do what is necessary to _____." And unless you are one of the few individuals who has a personal coach or a coachlike friend, no one will talk with you about your personal goals and your progress toward them. Consequently, most people are reactive in their use of personal time. Instead of allocating time to specific personal goals, they respond to demands on their time as problems and opportunities unfold.

So before you read any further, do three things:

1. Clarify your personal goals. Succinctly describe each goal in a written statement, as in this example:

Over the next twelve months, I aim to master the guitar to the point that I can perform the works of Fernando Sor, and pieces of similar complexity, with a high level of artistic merit.

I want to engage in a two week-long bonding experience with my grown children and their spouses this year. This might involve hiking in the Scottish Highlands or holding a family retreat at a lakeside cottage, or something similar of their choosing.

I want to have four to five hours of free time every weekend to either visit a museum, do some fishing, or pursue some other nonchore activity.

The Examined Life

Speaking through Socrates in *The Apology*, Plato gave us an important piece of philosophical wisdom: "The unexamined life is not worth living." Plato urged us not only to look carefully at *how* we conduct our lives but also to examine our *purposes*, or goals.

What are your personal goals? Are they aligned with your highest values? Do you ever think deeply about them? If your answer to the last question is, "No, I haven't thought about my goals—I'm too busy trying to keep up with all the things I have to do," then it's definitely time to start thinking about what's important to you. If you fail to do this, the months and years will slip by before you know it, and you will not have moved any closer to the things you truly value.

Here's a tip: Set aside two hours and do nothing but contemplate what you want most to achieve during the next three to five years. Do this in a peaceful place that is free of distractions. Have a pencil and paper handy to record your thoughts and conclusions. Revise those conclusions over subsequent weeks to make adjustments and crystallize your conclusions. Share your conclusions with a trusted friend, relative, or spouse—someone who knows you very well. Repeat this exercise, but this time with the aim of answering this question: "What changes must I make in my work and personal lives to achieve my highest personal goals?"

2. Prioritize your goals. You probably have more goals than you have time to devote to them, and this means that you must set priorities. Thus, in the example, the person may decide that going off on a two week-long adventure with his children has the highest priority, followed by regular, disciplined music practice. Having a four- to five-hour block for enriching experiences every weekend may be a "nice-to-have" goal but not something high on the list of personal priorities.

3. Determine what you must do (enabling goals) to achieve your highest priorities. In most cases, you will have to make a change on the working side of your life to achieve your personal goals.

Make Time for the Things That Matter

After you've identified and prioritized your personal goals, make time for them in your schedule. If, for example, two weeks away with your children during the coming six months has top priority, then schedule it. Discuss the plan with your children, gain consensus about the where and when of your trip, and then block that week off on your calendar. What? Your chosen vacation week will conflict with a commitment you've made to be at Sheila's fiftieth birthday party? Assuming that you cannot arrange an alternative time for the family vacation, send Sheila your regrets about missing the party. It's not a priority. Don't allow unimportant things—even *urgent* unimportant things—to crowd out the things that truly matter to you.

As at the office, don't schedule your personal time so tightly that you cannot respond to unanticipated events and opportunities. Leave open space here and there on your calendar. If you have inadequate open space, then begin keeping a log of how you currently spend your personal time, as described earlier in this book. Write down everything from the time you leave work until the time you go to bed. Do the same for weekends. A review of your log may indicate that you are wasting lots of time on activities that don't matter to you.

Unclutter Your Personal Life

Material things, commitments, and relationships on the personal side of your life all consume time. Some are worth the time, but others are not. Your available personal time will expand as you free yourself from the things, commitments, and relationships that add little value to your life.

Tips for Eliminating Time Wasters on the Home Front

Finding and eliminating time wasters from your personal life is very satisfying when you realize that every wasted hour you eliminate creates an equal amount of time for the things that you really want to do. Here are a few things you can do to gain extra hours:

- Do more things at one time. Are you running to the super-market three times each week? Smart meal planning could eliminate two of those three trips, saving one or two hours per week for you.

- Combine trips. If your activity log shows that you or other household members are making separate trips to the super-market, the dry cleaner, the post office, and so forth, consolidate those chores into one or two trips. A few minutes of planning and coordination may save you several more hours each week.

- Reduce television viewing. Television can be addicting, particularly for people who live alone. And let's face it, most TV programming is low-quality stuff, and almost one-third of airtime on the commercial channels is nothing more than a blitzkrieg of blaring advertisements. Compare the value of this programming with the value of your goals. Not much of a contest, is it? Consider junking the TV entirely. In this same vein, give some thought to your use of the Internet. It can be just as addicting as TV.

- Shop by catalog or the Internet. Some people will spend an entire afternoon driving to a shopping mall, wandering from store to store, and never finding what they set out for. In most cases they could have found exactly what they wanted in a direct-mail catalog or on the Internet in a half-hour or less, and the balance of the afternoon would belong to them.

Continued

> • Outsource. Heart surgeons don't take time from work or spend their limited free time fixing their plumbing or painting their houses. The reason is simple: They can hire someone who has the skills to do the job better and faster—and at a fraction of their own hourly billing rates. Every household has opportunities for this type of economical outsourcing. What are yours?

Reduce the Number of Things You Own

Whether you realize it or not, material possessions absorb time. Think for a moment about the amount of time you spend cleaning and maintaining your home, your automobile, and your household appliances. Even things that don't require maintenance, such as the pile of music CDs stacked on the kitchen counter or your collection of figurines, demand some attention—if only because they must be dusted or because they get in your way. Some people feel their personal lives expand as they divest themselves of material possessions. Their caretaker role diminishes, leaving time for other things. Think about how uncluttering your household of material things would give you more time for things you value.

Rein In Your Commitments

Commitments also absorb time. We all make commitments—to civic groups, friends, and family. Perhaps you've made a commitment to your church to run its annual fund-raiser, or to your neighbors to water their houseplants every week while they are wintering in southern France. Commitments are the social glue that bind families and communities together. But some of us agree to commitments too readily and without thinking of the impact they have on our time. This is no different from the overreaching problem described in chapter 4.

Tips for Getting Rid of Material Clutter

- Stop acquiring things. Stay away from shopping malls and other temptations to Buy! Buy! Buy!

- If you encounter something you simply must have, don't purchase it until you have identified something in your household that you will recycle, sell, or give away.

- Every so often, go around your house or apartment with an empty cardboard box. Fill it with things you haven't used for some time and don't expect to use soon. Label the box with the date and the items it contains. Put that box in storage for one year. When the year has gone by, get rid of anything you haven't retrieved from the box. If you never opened the box during the elapsed year, get rid of the entire box.

- Periodically give away things that will produce more satisfaction for others than they produce for you. This will eliminate things and make you feel good at the same time.

To keep personal commitments in line with time availability, periodically review the commitments you have made and determine whether they continue to make sense. Ask these questions:

- Is my commitment actually producing value—for me and for others?

- Are the benefits I receive (material or nonmaterial) from my commitments commensurate with the value I provide to others?

- Would ending my commitment produce harm to anyone?

- How much time will I gain by ending this commitment?

Relationships are a particular form of commitment, and like commitments made to civic groups and other organizations, they absorb time. One would hope that one's relationships are worth the time, because personal relationships are usually our most important source of meaning and satisfaction. Experience, however, indicates that not all relationships are worth the time we put into them. This is particularly true when the give-and-take implicit in relationships is lopsided—that is, when one party puts in much more time than does the other or when one party contributes little or nothing and yet receives most of the benefits. It is also true when a relationship is a source of conflict or reflects an unhealthy level of dependency. Both will drain you of time and emotional energy while returning little or nothing of true value.

So, as with your commitments, periodically evaluate personal relationships with the goal of determining which should be strengthened, which should be diminished, and which should be ended. After you have freed yourself of unsatisfactory relationships, you'll feel a weight lifted from you and you will have more time and more capacity for relationships that are healthy and satisfying.

Build Your Energy

Some people, particularly older people, have plenty of time on their hands, and yet they accomplish very little because they lack the energy to do things they would like to do. We see the same malaise among younger people who have grown inactive because of obesity or other health problems.

What is your energy level? Do you find yourself fading after lunch? Are you too tired to do the things you'd like to do after work? Do you drag yourself home from work, have dinner, and then watch television for the evening? If this describes you, you probably lack the energy to deal with the time you already have—or the added hours you could have through time management.

The antidote may be a long-term program to improve your physical fitness. Such a program should include a healthy diet, along with a balance of strength and endurance training. Start with a medical checkup. In contrast to others, people who eat sensibly and who are physically fit can draw on deeper reserves of energy and stamina in accomplishing their goals. They can work harder and longer with less effort than the less-fit, adding extra productive hours to their days; they can attack those hours with greater vitality. And it's never too late. Studies have shown conclusively that even elderly people can increase their fitness levels and muscular strength.

Seek Work–Life Balance

Thus far, this book has treated the workplace and the world outside it as two independent and unconnected spheres. It has given the impression that goals and time issues in each sphere can be addressed separately. This may be true for people who feel alienated from their work or who view work as a necessary evil from which they derive financial rewards but no personal satisfaction.

The idea of employee alienation had a certain cachet when much of our economy was based on dronelike factory work. In the post-industrial West, however, that economy has been largely eclipsed by service- and knowledge-based work, both of which draw heavily on the skills, judgment, and creativity of individual employees. Consequently, workplace alienation has given way to involvement in a very real sense for many people. Even on factory assembly lines, today's work teams are often empowered to determine their own production schedules, work independently on quality issues, and take responsibility for output. For many, this involvement is a source of personal satisfaction that blurs the traditional line of separation between work life and personal life. That blurring has created a new issue: Are the two important elements of our lives—work goals and personal goals—satisfactorily balanced?

Work–life balance was one of the hottest business topics in the United States before the 2000–2002 recession. Dozens of books and hundreds of articles were written on the subject. And despite the shock of recession-driven layoffs in the years that followed, it remains an issue that refuses to go away, and for two reasons. First, some companies are piling so much onto employees that people cannot possibly complete their assignments during the normal business day. They must arrive early, stay late, or take work home with them. To make matters worse, business travel keeps many away from family and friends for three to four nights each week. The inevitable result is that personal goals and relationships suffer. There is simply not enough time on the personal side of the ledger to get things done.

Second, work–life balance is an important ingredient in employee satisfaction and loyalty. Companies that help employees find ways to balance work requirements with personal goals are better able to attract and retain high-quality employees. This is particularly true for companies that employ highly skilled, highly educated people who enjoy substantial employment choices.

A study by the Ford Foundation sums up what many other researchers have found about the work–life issue: "Restructuring the way work gets done to address work-family integration can lead to positive, 'win-win' results—a more responsive work environment that takes employees' needs into account and yields significant bottom-line results."[2] If this is correct, then both employees and companies have a stake in work–life balance. Work–life balance isn't just a "feel-good" issue or an expensive perk. It translates into higher employee satisfaction and lower turnover.

How satisfactory is your work–life balance? Is work crowding out your capacity to pursue important personal goals? If it is, turn to chapter 8, which contains several things that you and your company can do to get things into an acceptable balance.

Summing Up

- As in the workplace, the personal side of time management begins with goals. Most people, however, are reactive to their use of personal time, responding to problems and opportunities as they unfold.

- As at work, keep an activity log to record how you actually spend your nonworking hours.

- Create more personal time by reducing TV viewing, combining trips, shopping by Internet or direct mail, and so forth.

- Outsource household chores that others can do more cheaply and better than you can.

- Material things absorb time and attention, so get rid of things that add little or no value to your life.

- Commitments are an important element of family and community life. Just keep them in line with your time budget. Periodically review your existing commitments to determine whether they continue to provide meaning and satisfaction. Do the same with your relationships. Avoid, reduce, or terminate commitments and relationships that are unsatisfactory or fail to produce value.

- Physical fitness will give you stamina and energy, allowing you to do things longer and with less effort. If you're not fit, do something about it.

- Work–life balance is an issue that refuses to go away. Companies that help employees achieve satisfactory work–life balance generally enjoy higher employee satisfaction and lower turnover.

What Companies Can Do to Help

Ideas for Improving Employee Time Management

Key Topics Covered in This Chapter

- *Reducing travel time and expense through technology*

- *Reining in the time spent on presentation graphics*

- *Helping employees expand available time through work–life balance*

RESPONSIBILITY FOR EFFECTIVE time management settles squarely on the shoulders of individual employees, managers, and executives. It's their time, and time is the "product" they sell to their employers in return for wages and benefits. The more productivity and effectiveness they can pack into their time, the more they can demand for it.

Although time management is ultimately the employee's responsibility, every company has an interest in its employees' effective use of time. And there are several things companies can do to help. This chapter touches on three of them.

Use Technology to Reduce Travel Time

Travel is often necessary. But, as described earlier in this book, even necessary travel creates huge costs, as measured in time and money. Think of all the time that you and other company employees spend getting from one business destination to another. And think of the cost of the associated meals and lodging. Individuals can save travel time and money by simply cutting back on wasteful or marginally effective journeys. Their individual efforts, however, can be leveraged by companywide initiatives that use technology as travel substitutes.

People have attempted to reduce business-related travel ever since airmail and long-distance phone service became available. Aside from these important advances, however, little progress was made on this front until the late 1980s. Videoconferencing and, more recently, Web conferencing technologies have vastly improved our ability to conduct business without the time and expense of travel. Videoconferencing technology can be used effectively for training, sales presentations, companywide announcements, the conduct of focus groups, and even crisis control. It requires special equipment and is usually conducted from a specially equipped conference room.

Web conferencing aims to serve the same purpose but requires little special equipment or space. WebEx dominates this field, with Microsoft's LiveMeeting not far behind. Web conferencing does save companies both time and money. As reported by *Barron's*, Emerson Electric estimates that it saved about $6 million during the first two years it used one of these services.[1] Using this technology, two or more people can view and share documents and, with the use of Web cameras, see each other on their PC monitors. These features make

The Increasing Popularity of Virtual Meetings

Business travel has always been a drag. The 9/11 terror attack on the United States, and the lengthy security checks that followed, made it even more unappetizing. Then there was the SARS outbreak, which made every air traveler wonder, "Is that person coughing in the seat behind me carrying the SARS virus?"

These concerns and technological advances have increased the popularity of videoconferencing and Web-based conferencing compared with traditional face-to-face meetings. A 2004 survey conducted by U.K.-based Wainhouse Research has documented the growing popularity of these new media. The survey indicated that face-to-face meetings declined about 12 percent in 2001–2004. During that same period, the number of meetings held via videoconferencing almost doubled, as did Web-based conferencing. The latter, which uses both an audio link and online displays of text and graphics, grew almost 40 percent between 2003 and 2004 alone.

SOURCE: "Being There," *Economist*, 15–21 May 2004, 63.

Web conferencing one of the most cost-effective and time-efficient tools available for conference calls, training, product demonstration, and collaboration between far-flung project team members.

Many companies are using video- and Web conferencing to stay in touch even as they cut back on travel time. Other large employers with continuous training programs—among them Dell Computer, Ernst & Young, and the U.S. Navy—are doing the same with online training. Among other benefits, online training makes learning available 24/7. That lets participants squeeze training into open periods in their schedules without displacing mission-critical tasks. It also eliminates an important source of work–life conflict: the days and evenings that some employees would otherwise have to spend away from home at training sessions. Online learning is not a total substitute for the give-and-take found in traditional classroom situations, but it has an important place, and many companies are shifting toward greater reliance on online learning.

What is your company doing to save time by replacing physical travel with video- and Web conferencing? If it hasn't yet done anything, it is time to begin. Start by doing the following:

- Learn the capabilities of video- and Web conferencing.

- Identify the most promising applications for your business—for example, meetings between project team members who are geographically dispersed.

- Collaborate with your information technology personnel to set up and run a few pilot conferences.

- Learn from pilot tests.

- Incorporate that initial learning into a large rollout.

These forms of communication can save your company time and money that would otherwise be spent on travel. But, like e-mail and telephony, they are not perfectly equivalent to in-person, face-to-face communication on which much trust and business-building depend. So use these new technologies judiciously. They are not a complete substitute for physical travel.

Rein In Presentation Graphics

Presentations—to the sales force, to employee teams, and to top management—are a regular feature of organizational life. Once upon a time, people who made stand-up presentations would augment their delivery with a handout sheet containing data or graphics. Others might employ a paper flip chart to display key points. Later, with the widespread introduction of overhead projectors, speakers enhanced their verbal presentations with hand-drawn graphs and bullet-point lists. These low-tech visual aids were effective and took almost no time to prepare, allowing speakers to focus their valuable time on the content of their presentations.

This has changed in the era of presentation graphics, or slide-ware. Today, armed with powerful slideware programs such as the ubiquitous PowerPoint, highly paid managers and staff personnel spend—many people would say waste—hours creating images of dubious merit, experimenting with various fonts and background colors, tweaking endlessly to capture just the right look, and all with the goal of impressing their audiences. Although having a highly polished and professional look is important when you're addressing investors, customers, and many other external groups, it is much less important for internal use.

Critic Edward R. Tufte, an emeritus professor at Yale University, has complained that this urge to create knockout slides "routinely disrupts, dominates, and trivializes content."[2] His charge is certainly true in many cases. Going overboard with slideware is an obvious waste of personnel time, a resource waste that companies can do something about through commonsense rules for presentation visuals.

Unfortunately, no ambitious manager or staffer will unilaterally end the contest of trying to trump everyone else's slide presentation. That's where management should step in. Management should insist that slides used for internal presentations be simple and subordinated to the message. That insistence alone will save many hours of employee time. A little training on the essentials of visual presentations will reinforce management's policy.

Facilitate Work–Life Balance

Many people find that they simply have too little time outside work to address their key personal goals. Perhaps you're one of them. The reason, in many cases, can be traced to company practices: long workdays, take-home assignments, paltry vacations, travel demands, and weekend e-mails from the boss.

People are pushing back against relentless encroachments on their personal time and are seeking ways to balance the two sides of their lives. But they cannot do it by themselves; their employers must collaborate. Some companies have gotten the message and are responding with programs designed to help their employees achieve better work–life balance. Helping employees achieve this balance appears to pay off in employee satisfaction, retention, and the ability to recruit new workers.

At first blush, you'd think that every concession toward work–life balance would represent a cost to the sponsoring company. After all, if a company were to announce that it would be cutting back on overnight travel days so that employees would have more evenings at home, its ability to coordinate far-flung activities or meet with customers in distant cities might be impaired. But as Stewart Friedman, Perry Christensen, and Jessica DeGroot explained in a widely read *Harvard Business Review* article, work–life balance does not have to be a zero-sum game:

> *[W]e have observed that a small but growing number of managers . . . operate under the assumption that work and personal life are not competing priorities but complementary ones. In essence, they've adopted a win-win philosophy. And it appears they are right: in the cases we have studied, the new approach has yielded tangible payoffs both for organizations and for individual employees.*[3]

These researchers offer three principles for breaking through the zero-sum game:

1. Make sure that employees understand business priorities, and encourage them to be equally clear about their personal priorities. The work of the organization must get done, and

work–life balance should not be an excuse for letting it slide. After everyone's cards are on the table, schedules and assignments can usually be arranged in ways that satisfy both sides.

2. Recognize and support employees as "whole people" who have important roles outside the workplace. Managers can deal with work–life conflict only if they understand and show some interest in the nonworking lives of their employees.

3. Continually experiment with how work gets done. Smart managers know that work processes must be periodically rethought and redesigned for greater efficiency and effectiveness. Work–life balance provides opportunities to experiment with these processes with the goal of making them better.

The following sections point to several things that companies and their employees are doing to achieve a satisfactory balance between the two sides of their lives: telework, flexible work scheduling, and a menu of time-saving perks.

Telework

Telework, or work done by employees in locations other than their regular offices, is facilitated by telecommunications and Internet capabilities. The International Telework Association & Council (ITAC) defines telework as "using telecommunications to do wherever you need to in order to satisfy client needs: whether it be from a home office, telework center, satellite office, a client's office, an airport lounge, a hotel room, the local Starbucks, or from your office to a colleague 10 floors down in the same building."[4] The ITAC estimates that some twenty-eight million U.S. employees were involved in some form of telework in 2001.

Proponents of telework point to measurable cost savings and benefits to sponsoring companies, including lower real estate costs, greater employee productivity, greater employee loyalty and job satisfaction, and less personnel turnover. And the teleworkers themselves report that it helps them balance work and personal responsibilities. If they work from a home office one or more days each week, they can

Tips on Achieving Work–Life Balance

Here are a few things that managers can do to make work–life balance a win-win situation:

- Give more attention to results than to how, where, and when the work gets done. Say, "You are responsible for conducting a customer survey and producing a complete report between now and mid-March. I'd like you to develop a plan for handling that."

- Get to know your employees and coworkers on a personal level. Do they have civic obligations that need tending to? Do they have children or aging parents to support? What hobbies or artistic pursuits absorb their attention? Do they have other skills that might benefit the company? As the famous Hawthorne experiments found many decades ago, making these inquiries and simply *showing an interest* in employees as individuals can have a positive impact on morale and motivation.

- Encourage people to find new and better ways of meeting their responsibilities. For example, sales managers and product development people may discover that a $5,000 investment in videoconferencing equipment could save the company $15,000 each year in travel expenses—and save each of them weeks of unproductive travel time and many nights away from home. Supervisors may find that their 4:00 p.m. staff meetings—the ones that never seem to end before 6:30 p.m. and make everyone late for dinner—could easily be rescheduled as a lunch meeting. That would get the job done *and* get people home on time.

dramatically cut one of the big-time drains of modern urban life: commuting time. That is time that employees can allocate to personal goals. Home-based telework also makes it possible for parents to be on the premises when their children return from school, an important issue for working parents.

AT&T, which has used telework heavily since the early 1990s, conducted a random survey in 2000 of 1,238 managers and found clear evidence of positive benefits for itself and teleworkers:

- Teleworkers actually put in more hours. Respondents indicated that they worked at least one hour more per day; that's equivalent to two hundred fifty hours, or six weeks, of extra (unpaid) work done by the average teleworker. But those workers saved time for themselves by reducing commuting times.

- Telework is more productive. Some 77 percent of AT&T's teleworkers said that they got more accomplished at home than they did in the office.

- Loyalty improves. Of those teleworkers who reported receiving competing job offers, 67 percent said that giving up the telework environment was a factor in their decision to turn down those offers.

- Attracting and retaining good employees are made easier, according to 66 percent of responding AT&T managers.

- Since shifting to telework, 77 percent of teleworkers are more satisfied with their careers.

- Achieving work–life balance is easier. Some 83 percent of AT&T teleworkers reported being more satisfied with their personal and family lives since beginning telework arrangements.

AT&T also reported saving $25 million annually in real estate costs because its full-time teleworkers required neither work nor parking spaces at company locations.[5]

These remarkable findings are not unique to AT&T. But before your company or business unit adopts a telework program, it should think through a number of questions:

- Which jobs are appropriate for telework?

- What are the legal, regulatory, insurance, and technology issues? (Individual stockbrokers, for example, cannot work from an unsupervised office of a broker-dealer.)

- How will teleworkers be supervised to ensure accountability?

- Will people worry that telework will negatively affect their chances for promotions and other recognition?

Despite claims on its behalf, however, telework is not appropriate for every organization or individual. In an article for the *Harvard Business Review*, Mahlon Apgar addressed this question, explaining that programs such as telework are most appropriate when companies are

- committed to new ways of operating

- more informational than industrial

- dynamic, nonhierarchical, technologically advanced

Telework Readiness

Are you a good candidate for telework? How about subordinates who've been asking you for permission to work from home every Friday? AT&T's telework advice site has a handy "Personnel Screener" that will evaluate the readiness of any employee for telework. That automated screener evaluates telework readiness in four dimensions:

1. **Prerequisites.** Levels of job knowledge, experience, productivity, work quality, and so on.
2. **Skills.** The ability to plan and manage projects, to set and reach goals, and so on.
3. **Work style.** The ability to work with a minimum of supervision, the ability to work independently, and so on.
4. **Attitude factor.** A willingness to try new things, a positive attitude toward telework, and so on.

This self-diagnostic test helps individuals identify their strengths as well as any barriers they might need to overcome before trying telework.

SOURCE: www.att.com/telework/get_started/gs_perscr.html

- not command-driven

- willing to invest in tools and training.[6]

Telework also requires adaptation on the part of managers and supervisors. After all, if their charges are not under their watchful eyes, how can a manager know whether subordinates are working or watching *Seinfeld* reruns? The remedy, according to most experts, is for managers to focus on results instead of activities. That means setting clear goals for individual teleworkers, making sure that they understand those goals, and setting up a system for monitoring progress in short-term stages. Managers must also find ways to integrate teleworkers into the larger group; otherwise, people may become isolated and out of touch and not feel part of the team.

Could telework help you regain time lost to commuting and use that time to address your personal goals? Would it cause your work performance to improve or suffer? Would it jeopardize opportunities for advancement? These are important questions that you must answer.

Flexible Work Schedules

Flexible scheduling is another mechanism that companies can adopt to help employees achieve work–life balance. Flexible scheduling allows individual employees to break out of the traditional 9-to-5, forty-hour, five-day week. It creates opportunities for people to work even as they accommodate the needs of young children, infirm relatives, and so forth.

Many people favor flexible schedules. This is what the accounting and consulting firm Deloitte & Touche learned when it surveyed its professional staff—both men and women—in 1993. Four-fifths (80 percent) said that they wanted greater flexibility in where, how, and when they worked. The company responded the next year with programs for both flexible work arrangements and parental leave. By 2000, approximately nine hundred of the firm's professional employees were enrolled in at least one of these programs.[7]

Time Management Tips for Home-Based Work

People who spend one or more days per week working from home immediately reap a time dividend equal to the time they would waste commuting to the office. This typically adds one to three hours to the day—a real windfall!

However, that dividend is easily squandered if home workers don't protect themselves from interruptions, particularly from distractions and from people who unwittingly show no respect for the fact that they are working. People who work from home are repeatedly asked by family members to handle chores. These family members simply don't think of home-based work as real work and feel that the home worker is always available to deal with household issues. "You're at home today. Could you pick up my suit from the dry cleaner?" "Aunt Sarah has a two-o'clock appointment with her doctor. Will you give her a ride?"

Here are a few antidotes to these requests:

- Keep regular home-office hours, and insist that others respect them. A family meeting on this matter is a good way to get the issue on the table. Use that meeting to explain why your time must be respected.

- Include some flexibility. Flexibility is, after all, one of the benefits of home-based work. So indicate times during the day when you are available for chores—for example, during your lunch break.

- Install a separate office phone. Allow the answering machine to pick up calls to your home phone.

- Have a separate area for doing home–based work—preferably a separate room with a door.

If you follow these tips, your commuting dividend time will not evaporate.

Did these programs help retain professional employees? Clearly, they did. Some 80 percent of the individuals enlisted in the Deloitte & Touche programs reported that they would have left the firm if the programs had not been made available. If you figure the average replacement cost of seven hundred twenty Deloitte & Touche professionals at 1.5 times annual salary (assumed here at $75,000), the savings to the firm are roughly $81 million. Improved retention indicates that employees valued flexibility.

Here are some typical flex-schedule arrangements:

- **Reduced-time schedules.** For example, an employee works from 10 to 6 in order to drive children to school in the morning.

- **Seasonal schedules.** For example, a tax specialist works sixty-hour weeks from January through April to accommodate the tax-filing deadline and then works thirty-hour weeks for the balance of the year.

- **Compressed schedules.** For example, to accommodate his weekend acting vocation, a computer technician puts in forty hours Monday through Thursday, leaving Fridays free for rehearsals. This serves both a personal goal and his workplace goals.

Flexible work schedules are appreciated by many employees, particularly people more than fifty years old. Life seems shorter at fifty-plus. With much to do and little time in which to do it, personal goals gradually gain in importance compared with workplace goals. People begin to joke that no one on his deathbed ever said, "I only wish that I'd spent more time at work." They begin to think of the personally fulfilling things they want to do: travel, spend time with grandchildren, pursue hobbies, and so forth. Flex-time, job sharing, sabbaticals, and unpaid vacation days are options that older employees should consider using to deal with the changing importance of workplace and personal goals. Companies that want to retain the skills and experience of these older workers should find ways to oblige them.

Time–Saving Perks

Some companies have instituted perks that give every employee a chance to handle personal chores at work that would otherwise absorb scarce personal time. These include the following:

- **On–site day care.** Many companies now offer on–site day care for employees. Instead of making separate trips to their children's care providers before and after work, employees with preschool children can simply bring them to work, where day care is provided on the premises. They can even visit their children during lunch. High–quality, on–site day care is popular with employees and an excellent recruiting and retention tool.

- **On–site medical care.** Have you ever wasted half a day visiting your doctor's office because you needed a blood test or a throat culture? Lots of waiting. Lots of driving. Software giant SAS is one of several companies that have eliminated this type of time waster by establishing small health clinics right on their business premises. This is an expensive proposition, but a company with a large campuslike facility can take it in stride.

- **Concierge services.** If you are like most people, you have to make extra trips on your own time to the shoe repair shop, the film processing shop, the post office, and the dry cleaner. And every so often you have to stop on the way home to pick up a warm-and-serve dinner. Think of the time you would save each week if you could handle those chores in the lobby of your building. Some large employers are arranging for these types of on–site service. It can be done at no cost to the company.

Company-sponsored arrangements like these help employees with work–life balance, even when their employers demand long workdays. What could your company be doing that would produce the same benefit without costing too much?

Teach Time–Management Principles

Let's suppose that you took the advice offered in this book to heart and managed your time more carefully. How much of your time would be freed up for high-priority activities—10 percent? 20 percent? 30 percent? Even a 10 percent improvement would make you noticeably more productive, right? Now, what would happen if *everyone* in your company made similar improvements?

Simply put, you'd have a more efficient and more effective organization. Meetings would be shorter and more productive. Far fewer expensive overnight trips would be taken. Tasks would take less time to complete. People wouldn't busy themselves with activities that did not advance the company's goals. Best of all, people would be completing their work by the normal quitting time and not dragging it home. The results of these improvements would find their way to the bottom line in increased output per employee.

Many companies attempt to create this ideal state through time-management training, which is often delivered by outside vendors through either online learning or traditional seminars. Some vendors have separate programs for senior managers and rank-and-file employees. Those offered to senior people and to unit heads are highly customized and focus heavily on goal alignment within the organization. The emphasis in these cases is on ensuring that people at all levels are working on the right things.

Less senior people and the rank and file are more apt to receive a standard curriculum that covers the topics found in the first four chapters of this book—one that focuses on goals, differentiating between what is important and what is simply urgent, analysis of time-use habits, and ways to eliminate time robbers. Some companies have even hired consultants to work one-on-one with people experiencing unusual time-management problems. Whichever approach is taken, training in time-management methods can change people's behavior for the better, but only if they recognize the problem and want to improve.

Make Time Management a Habit

Most time-management training is administered in a two- to three-hour seminar, and trainers know from experience that only a small part of what they communicate will "stick." People walk out of the training room with every intention of managing their time more effectively. And they may even take the first steps: filling out activity logs and thinking through their goals. But few people change their behavior in the absence of periodic reinforcement and practice. The same is true of people who read time-management books such as this one. Reinforcement helps the important concepts to stick, and practice makes a habit of positive behavior change.

So if you or your subordinates have just finished a company-sponsored time-management seminar, you and they need to turn what you've learned into improved habits. And everything said next applies to the things you have learned in this book. You can do this by doing the following:

- Talking with each other about the concepts you've learned

- Keeping an activity log and analyzing time use

- Thinking and talking about goals

- Developing a schedule and to-do list

- Being aware of your personal time wasters and finding ways to defeat them

- Transferring what you've learned about time management at work to the home front

The final thing you must do is evaluate your time-management performance and seek continuous improvement. This means periodically stepping outside yourself and critiquing your time-use habits:

- Are my goals still important?

- Is my schedule under- or overloaded?

- Is most of my time spent on critical and enabling goals, or have I fallen prey to the urgent but unimportant?

- Have I defeated any of my usual time robbers?

Use the answers to these questions to plan for improved performance. If you are a manager, help your subordinates make more of the time they have. You'll be helping them and yourself in equal measure.

Time management is a personal responsibility, but companies can help. This chapter has explained how. In the end, companies whose people are efficient and effective in their use of time are bound to outpace rivals whose employees allow time to slip through their fingers.

Summing Up

- Companies can help their personnel save substantial amounts of time by making judicious use of the latest travel substitutes: videoconferencing and Web conferencing.

- Companywide communication, training, product demonstrations, and team-based work can all benefit from videoconferencing and Web conferencing.

- Some managers and staff personnel spend many hours trying to produce presentation slides with all the right fonts, colors, and other features. This is seldom necessary for internal presentation. Companies should encourage these people to save time by using simpler slides.

- Work–life balance is an important issue for employees. Long workdays, take-home assignments, short vacations, and travel demands—all company-controlled features of the workplace—contribute to the problem.

- Companies can help employees find a satisfying work–life balance through programs involving telework, flexible scheduling, and a menu of time-saving perks, such as on-site day care, health, and concierge services.

- Companies have a compelling interest in the time-management skills of their employees, managers, and executives. Company-sponsored training in time-management skills can create a win-win situation.

- Time-management training has little impact in the absence of reinforcement and continual improvement. People become good time managers only when they practice it and review their progress. Sitting through a two-hour seminar is unlikely to produce real improvements.

Useful Implementation Tools

This appendix contains a number of tools that can help you be more effective in managing your time. All the forms are adapted from Harvard ManageMentor®, an online product of Harvard Business School Publishing. Readers can freely access other worksheets, checklists, and interactive tools found on the Harvard Business Essentials Web site: www.elearning.hbsp.org/businesstools.

1. **Daily Activity Log Chart (figure A-1).** Complete the log to record your daily activities. Use the first three columns to record actual time, activity, and time used. For each activity, check off the corresponding category.

2. **Goals Worksheet (figure A-2).** Use this worksheet to identify and prioritize your goals. Remember: Critical goals are goals essential to your success. They must be accomplished in order for your business or your unit to continue running successfully. Enabling goals create a more desirable business condition or take advantage of a business opportunity. Nice-to-have goals make business-enhancing improvements. They usually relate to making activities faster, easier, or more pleasant.

3. **Schedule Evaluation Checklist (figure A-3).** It is important to periodically review the effectiveness of your scheduling technique. This checklist takes you through a set of self-diagnostic questions that help you improve scheduling on a regular basis. Check your progress against your schedule at least once a day.

FIGURE A-1

Daily Activity Log Chart

Date

				Category			
Time	Activity	Time Used (Minutes)	Telephone Calls	Scheduled Appointments	Drop-in/ Ad Hoc Meetings	Meetings	Paperwork

Source: Harvard ManageMentor® on Time Management, adapted with permission.

FIGURE A-2

Goals Worksheet

Goal	Priority	Comment

Source: Harvard ManageMentor® on Time Management, adapted with permission.

Appendix A

Schedule Evaluation Checklist

Question	Yes	No
Are you completing the tasks you set for the week? *If no, action strategies to implement:*		
Are you making progress on achieving your goals? *If no, perhaps you are scheduling too many activities. Review the activities on your schedule and eliminate any that do not support your top-priority goals. Activities to eliminate:*		
Do you feel better prepared and focused? *If no, action strategies to implement:*		
Was there an impact for not doing some tasks? *If yes, action strategies to implement next time:*		
Are you avoiding time wasters? *If no, look for other solutions by asking colleagues how they deal with this issue. Maybe your initial strategies were unrealistic, but can be modified. Other solutions:*		
Is this a schedule you can keep up? *If no, action strategies to implement:*		
What sources of support (including peer or supervisory support) can you enlist to help manage your schedule?		

Source: Harvard ManageMentor® on Time Management, adapted with permission.

Work Breakdown Structure

Big goals are difficult to deal with directly. It is hard to know where to begin. The best way to deal with big goals is to break them into smaller, more manageable tasks. When you have accomplished each of the tasks, you'll have accomplished the goal. This is exactly what project managers do when they construct skyscrapers, design new aircraft, and create even intangible things such as e-commerce Web sites.

This appendix explains how you can use the concept of a work breakdown structure (WBS) to approach large goals. Using a WBS and starting with the top objective, you can decompose the project goal into the many tasks required to achieve it. From a time-management perspective, this approach can help you answer these key questions:

- What must I do to achieve my goal?

- How long will it take?

- What will it cost?

Project managers use a WBS to develop estimates, assign personnel, track progress, and reveal the scope of project work. You can use this tool to subdivide complex tasks into many smaller tasks. These tasks, in turn, can usually be broken down still further.

To create a WBS, ask this question: What must be done to accomplish my objective? By asking that same question repeatedly for each task and subtask, you will eventually reach a point at which tasks cannot be further subdivided. Consider this example:

ABC Auto Company plans to introduce a new passenger car. This is a big, big job. At the highest level, its employees are faced with four tasks:

1. Determine customer-focused requirements.

2. Design a vehicle that will meet those requirements.

3. Construct the vehicle.

4. Test the vehicle.

As figure B-1 indicates, each of those top-level tasks can be broken down into a set of subtasks. And each of the subtasks shown in the figure can be broken down still further. For example, engine schematics, under the vehicle design task, can be decomposed into dozens of subtasks, such as transmission system design and cooling system design.

FIGURE B-1

Work Breakdown Structure

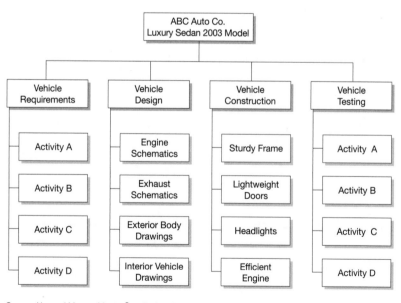

Source: Harvard ManageMentor® on Project Management, adapted with permission.

In this example, the project team for the new vehicle will eventually reach a point where there is no practical reason to break tasks down further. That point may be when tasks are decomposed into manageable one-week or one-day increments. At that point, work breakdown ends.

A WBS typically consists of three to six levels of subdivided activities. The more complex the project, the more levels it will have. As a rule, you should stop subdividing tasks when you reach the point where the work will take the smallest time unit you plan to schedule. Thus, if you want to schedule to the nearest day, break down the work to the point where each task takes a day to perform.

After you are satisfied with the breakdown of tasks, you must answer a new set of questions:

- How much time will it take to complete each task?

- What will be the likely cost of completing each task?

- What skills will be needed to complete each task well?

Because this book is about time management, let's address only the first of these questions.

A good time estimate for each task will help you schedule your work. If a task is familiar—that is, it's something you or others have done many times before—it isn't difficult to estimate completion time. Unfamiliar tasks, in contrast, require much more thinking and discussion. Just remember that these time estimates will eventually be rolled up into a schedule for the entire goal (or project), so you want to be as realistic as possible. Grossly underestimating the time component will come back to haunt you later. Here are a few tips for making these time estimates:

- Estimates should be based on experience, using the average expected time to perform a task. The more familiar you or other employees are with a particular task, the more accurate your estimate will be.

- Always remember that estimates are just that—estimates. They're not guarantees, so don't change them into firm commitments at this phase.

- Padding estimates is an acceptable way of reducing the risk that a task (or the entire project) will take longer than the schedule allows. But this practice should be done openly and with full awareness of what you're doing.

You've learned only the basics of creating a work breakdown structure. If you'd like to learn more or learn how to break down tasks for project management purposes, see *Harvard Business Essentials: Managing Projects Large and Small.*

A Guide to Effective Meetings

Meetings are a fact of life in most organizational work. Because meetings are frequent and important, it's in your interest to make meetings as effective as possible.

You can conduct effective meetings if you pay attention to these key aspects of meetings: preparation, the meeting process, and follow-up. This guide is adapted from Harvard ManageMentor®, an online product of Harvard Business School Publishing.

Be Prepared

You've undoubtedly attended meetings for which there was little or no preparation. Did those meetings accomplish anything? Probably not. In some cases, the purpose of the meeting was unclear from the beginning. In others, one or more of the people needed to make a decision didn't receive an invitation. You can avoid such mistakes by following these commonsense rules:

- Make sure that your meetings are necessary. Meetings eat up time for everyone at the table. If you can accomplish your objective without calling a meeting, do so.

- Clarify every meeting's objective. Every attendee should be able to answer this question: Why am I here? If the objective is to make a decision, be sure that everyone understands this in advance, and make sure that they have the time and materials needed to prepare.

- Involve the right people. Invite only those who have something to contribute, whose participation is necessary, or who can learn from the discussion.

- Provide an agenda in advance. An agenda indirectly identifies the meeting's objective.

- Sound out key participants in advance. You'll be better prepared for a meeting if you know in advance what key participants think about important items on the agenda. What you learn may suggest an alteration in the agenda.

- Insist that people be prepared. This means being up to speed on the issues; bringing relevant documents, reports, or physical objects; and being ready to contribute to the discussion and a decision.

Figure C-1 shows a checklist that comes in handy when you're planning a meeting.

During the Meeting

Good preparation will set you up for this second stage. Here you should do the following:

- State the meeting's purpose. Even though you said it when you invited people to the meeting, it's always smart to reiterate the meeting's purpose.

- Let everyone have a say. If one or two individuals are dominating the conversation, or if certain attendees are shy about leaping in, say, "Thanks for those ideas, Phil. What are your thoughts about this problem, Charlotte?"

- Keep the discussion from wandering. Meetings that wander off the key issues quickly degenerate into time-wasting gab sessions.

FIGURE C-1

Meeting Planner's Checklist

Use this checklist to be sure that you have covered all the important steps in preparing for an effective meeting.

Have You?	Yes	No	Notes
1. Identified the purpose of the meeting?			
2. Identified the objectives of the meeting?			
3. Selected the participants and identified roles?			
4. Identified the decision-making process (e.g., group leader, attendees, another manager)?			
5. Decided where and when to hold the meeting and confirmed availability of the space?			
6. Identified and confirmed availability of any needed equipment?			
7. Notified participants of when and where?			
8. Developed a preliminary agenda with purpose and objectives?			
9. Sent preliminary agenda to key participants and other stakeholders to sound them out in advance?			
10. Finalized the agenda and distributed it to all participants?			
11. Sent any reports or items needing preparation to participants?			
12. Verified that all key people will attend?			
13. Prepared yourself (e.g., handouts, overheads, etc.)?			

Source: Harvard ManageMentor® on Running a Meeting, adapted with permission.

• End with confirmation and an action plan. Your meeting should transition to some action. "Okay, we've decided to hire DataWhack to install the new servers. And, as agreed, I will obtain the purchase order, Bill will phone the salesperson and set up the schedule, and Janet will begin looking for someone to take the old equipment off our hands."

Meeting Leaders Wear Many Hats

If you are leading a meeting, you must wear many hats. Depending on the dynamics within the group, the leader must sometimes perform the following duties:

• **Gatekeeper.** You ensure that the agenda is followed, that everyone who wants to speak gets the opportunity, and that no one dominates. This is a tough job when you have a domineering individual at the table.

• **Devil's advocate.** You challenge a consensus that may be emerging prematurely—that is, without sufficient thought. Because people are social animals, opinion tends to converge as people discuss things. It's against most people's nature to hold out against the thinking of the majority. When you see this happening, take an opposing point of view, if only to force people to examine their assumptions and their willingness to agree.

• **Consensus builder.** You spot and highlight areas of agreement among members. Consensus building is necessary when people cannot or will not seek common ground.

• **Cheerleader.** In this role, you give genuine praise to members when it is due. Everyone likes to be appreciated.

• **Joker.** You relieve tension and remind members of common bonds.

The next time you attend a well-run meeting, observe how the leader or chairperson plays one or more of these roles.

Follow–Up

After a meeting is over, we're all tempted to relax and say, "I'm glad that's over with." But it isn't over if you led the meeting or agreed to accept responsibility for actions emanating from it.

The meeting leader should rapidly follow up with a quick memo in this spirit:

From: Richard
To: The IT Project Team

Thanks for your contributions to this morning's meeting. We have selected DataWhack as the supplier for the new servers. I view this as a good choice and a decision that moves us one step closer to the completion of our project. The action steps from this decision are as follows:

- *I will obtain the purchase order.*

- *Bill will contact the salesperson about the schedule.*

- *Janet will begin looking for someone to take the old servers off our hands.*

Let's complete these chores this week. Then we can get on to the next scheduled task.

This type of follow-up memo encourages people by saying that they are one step closer to their goal, and it reminds certain attendees about the action steps to which they have agreed.

Notes

Introduction

1. Human innovation in the segmentation of time is nicely described by Daniel J. Boorstin in *The Discoverers* (New York: Vintage Books, 1985), 26–46.

2. James Gleick, *Faster: The Acceleration of Just About Everything* (New York: Vintage Books, 2000), 15.

3. George Stalk Jr. and Thomas M. Hout, *Competing Against Time* (New York: The Free Press, 1990), 1.

4. Henry Mintzberg, "The Manager's Job: Folklore and Fact," *Harvard Business Review,* March–April 1990: 164, 169.

Chapter 1

1. Parts of this chapter have been adapted from the Goals module of Harvard ManageMentor®, an online program of Harvard Business School Publishing.

2. George Labovitz and Victor Rosansky, *Alignment* (New York: John Wiley & Sons, Inc, 1997), 4–5.

Chapter 2

1. For a concise treatment of Franklin's approach to the thirteen virtues, along with a modern rendering of his notebook pages for tracking his progress in each, visit "Suggestions for Living Better from the Life of Benjamin Franklin," by John R. Fisher, <www.fisherhouse .com/books/virtues.PDF> (accessed 16 June 2004).

Chapter 4

1. William Oncken Jr. and Donald Wass, "Management Time: Who's Got the Monkey?" *Harvard Business Review,* November–December 1999.

2. David Ferris and Ben Gross, "The Time Overhead of Email," Report #398, Ferris Research, San Francisco, CA, December 2003, 16.

3. See Melissa Raffoni, "How to Be Sure You're Spending Your Time in the Right Places," *Harvard Management Update,* October 2001, 8.

Chapter 5

1. This chapter has adapted material found in the Delegating module of Harvard ManageMentor®, an online product of Harvard Business School Publishing.

Chapter 6

1. John J. Gabarro and John P. Kotter, "Managing Your Boss," *Harvard Business Review,* May–June 1993, 157.

Chapter 7

1. Juliet Schor, *The Overworked American* (New York: Basic Books, 1998), 12.

2. Rhona Rapaport and Lotte Bailyn, "Relinking Life and Work," The Ford Foundation, <www.fordfound.org> (accessed 13 April 2004).

Chapter 8

1. Eric C. Fleming, "What Next for WebEx," *Barron's,* 15 June 2004.

2. Edward R. Tufte, "PowerPoint Is Evil," *Wired,* Issue 11.09, September 2003, <www.wired.com/wired/archive/11.09/ppt2.html> (accessed 18 May 2004).

3. Stewart D. Friedman, Perry Christensen, and Jessica DeGroot, "Work and Life: The End of the Zero Sum Game," *Harvard Business Review* 76, no. 6 (November–December 1998): 119–129.

4. See the ITAC Web site at <www.telecommute.org> for its definition of telework and its research findings.

5. See <www.att.com/telework> for AT&T's research on telework. The site also includes many articles on this subject as well as a "getting started" guide to implementing telework programs and policies.

6. Mahlon Apgar IV, "The Alternative Workplace: Changing Where and How People Work," *Harvard Business Review* 76, no. 3 (May–June 1998): 121–136.

7. See <www.deloitte.com/more/women/wiar/movie.html>.

Glossary

ACTIVITY LOG An accurate chronology of how each moment of the workday was spent. For time-management purposes, an activity log should be developed for each of three consecutive days.

BOTTLENECK BOSS A superior who acts as a pinch-point in the work flow, causing work to back up. This practice wastes time for employees, who must wait to complete their tasks.

CRITICAL GOALS Goals that are essential to your success. They must be accomplished in order for your business or your unit to continue running successfully.

DELEGATION The assignment of a specific task or project by one person to another, and the assignee's commitment to complete the task or project. Delegation is not only the transfer of work to another person but also transfer of accountability for completing that work to a stated standard.

ENABLING GOALS Goals that create a more desirable business condition or take advantage of a business opportunity. They are important but fill a long-term, rather than immediate, need. In a sense they facilitate the achievement of critical goals.

GOAL SETTING A formal process of defining outcomes worth achieving.

NICE-TO-HAVE GOALS Goals that make business-enhancing improvements. They usually relate to making activities faster, easier, or more pleasant.

PROCRASTINATION The habit of delaying or putting off doing something that should be done now.

SWITCHING COST Following a distraction or interruption, the time cost incurred when people review what they've done before they can resume work on a task.

TIME MANAGEMENT A conscious attempt to control and allocate finite time resources.

WORK BREAKDOWN STRUCTURE (WBS) A tool that project managers use to develop estimates, assign personnel, track progress, and reveal the scope of project work. This tool is used to subdivide complex tasks into many smaller tasks. These tasks, in turn, can usually be broken down still further.

For Further Reading

Books

Allen, David. *Getting Things Done: The Art of Stress-Free Productivity*. New York: Penguin Group, 2003 (paperback edition). Allen's premise is that personal productivity is proportional to one's ability to relax. A clear, stress-free mind is the starting point for personal productivity. One highlight of Allen's books is a flow chart that shows how to handle the dozens of tasks and communications that hit our e-mail and physical in-baskets every day.

Covey, Stephen R. *First Things First*. New York: Free Press, 1996 (paperback edition). Cowritten with Roger and Rebecca Merrill, this book emerged from Covey's landmark *The Seven Habits of Highly Effective People*. Habit 3 in that book, "Put first things first," is about personal time management. This book expands on what Covey had to say about that particular habit, describing a system based on a four-quadrant approach that urges people to view their tasks as belonging to these categories:

1. Important and urgent. These apply to crises and deadline-driven tasks with high priorities.

2. Important, not urgent. These are the bread and butter of managerial life: preparation, prevention, planning, and people-tending.

3. Urgent, not important. Many people unwittingly fill their days with tasks that belong in this category.

4. Not urgent, not important. This quadrant includes the irredeemable time wasters that clutter many lives.

The book presents an entire system for organizing what the authors describe as four human needs and capacities: to live, to love, to learn, and to leave a legacy. In this sense it takes a whole-person approach that encourages people to create a mission, balance work and home roles, build relationships, and focus on the things that matter in the long run. Some readers are bound to view this system as too rigid and demanding.

Loehr, Jim, and Tony Schwartz. *The Power of Full Engagement*. New York: Free Press, 2003. For these authors, energy, and not time, is the fundamental currency of high performance. This makes the book much different from—and yet a useful companion to—any program of traditional time management.

The authors identify four key sources of energy: spiritual, mental, emotional, and physical. In dealing with these sources, readers are urged to balance energy expenditures with periodic energy renewal—through rest, concentration, meditation, and so forth—just as trained athletes do. The authors also describe ways to *increase* energy capacity, allowing a person to do more in the same amount of time.

Many of the concepts detailed in this interesting book can be found in "The Making of the Corporate Athlete," a *Harvard Business Review* article written in 2001 by the same authors. See the later section on articles.

Mackenzie, Alec. *The Time Trap*. 3rd Edition. New York: AMACOM, 1997. The granddaddy of time-management books, Mackenzie's treatment is traditional—but still effective. Readers with specific problems may wish to refer to Part Two of this book: "The Twenty Biggest Time Wasters and How to Cure Them."

Merrill, Rebecca, and A. Roger. *Life Matters: Creating a Dynamic Balance of Work, Family, Time & Money*. New York: McGraw-Hill, 2003. The authors provide a guide to achieving harmony among one's life commitments, drawing on Stephen Covey's work in time and life management and his four-quadrant system for organizing daily activities. They offer perspectives on integrating family issues into goal setting and developing an inner sense of direction to keep oneself on track from one day to the next. Among the subjects covered are

- the gap between what people value and the reality of their lives
- how to align resources with goals and values
- integrating work and personal life.

Munter, Mary. *Guide to Managerial Communication,* 6th edition. Upper Saddle River, NJ: Prentice Hall, 2004. This book suggests that a great deal of time is wasted by managers and staff personnel on the preparation of unnecessarily elaborate presentation slides. This book contains a very good section on the design and use of presentation visual aids, with an emphasis on simplicity and effectiveness. If you'd like clear models for presenting qualitative and quantitative information, Munter's chapter on visual aids is essential reading.

Speilman, Sue, and Liz Winfeld. *The Web Conferencing Book.* New York: AMACOM, 2003. Web conferencing is a cost-effective and time-saving substitute for traditional business travel. Companies are learning how to use it for meetings, product presentations, training, companywide communications, and collaborative work. This book is a practical introduction to the uses of Web conferences and the technical issues they involve, including employee training, equipment, and software.

Articles

Ashkenas, Ronald N., and Robert H. Schaffer, "Managers Can Avoid Wasting Time." *Harvard Business Review,* May–June 1982. Although much is made of improving productivity in general, managers should focus periodically on their own personal productivity. The problem of poor managerial productivity is enormous, say these authors, because most cures focus on the symptoms: long meetings, unnecessary telephone calls, and tasks that could be turned over to subordinates. Beneath these symptoms lies the disease: managers' anxiety, which comes with tackling innovative activities. These authors have discovered that three requirements of executives' jobs—organizing day-to-day activities, improving performance under pressure, and getting subordinates to be productive—cause so much anxiety that many managers retreat to performing routine tasks they already know how to do. The authors show how organizational environments permit executives to be unproductive and describe a strategy that can help them escape these time traps.

Bruch, Heike, and Sumantra Ghoshal, "Beware the Busy Manager." *Harvard Business Review*, February 2002. Managers will tell you that the resource they lack most is time. If you watch them, you'll see them rushing from meeting to meeting, checking their e-mail constantly, fighting fires—an astonishing amount of fast-moving activity that allows almost no time for reflection. Managers think they are attending to important matters, but they're really just spinning their wheels.

Over a ten-year period, authors Bruch and Ghoshal studied the behavior of busy managers, and their findings are frightening: Fully 90 percent of managers squander their time in all sorts of ineffective activities.

The authors argue that effective action relies on a combination of two traits: focus—the ability to zero in on a goal and see the task through to completion—and energy: the vigor that comes from intense personal commitment. Focus without energy devolves into listless execution or leads to burnout. Energy without focus, on the other hand, dissipates into the aimless busyness of wasteful failures. Using a two-by-two matrix, the authors plot these traits and, in doing so, create a useful framework for understanding the productivity levels of different managers. This article will help you identify where you fit on their focus–energy matrix.

Loehr, Jim, and Tony Schwartz. "The Making of a Corporate Athlete." *Harvard Business Review,* January 2001, 120–128. Management theorists have long sought to identify precisely what makes some people flourish under pressure and others fold. But they have come up with only partial answers: rich material rewards, the right culture, management by objectives. The problem with most approaches is that they deal with people only from the neck up, connecting high performance primarily with cognitive capacity. Authors Loehr and Schwartz argue that a successful approach to sustained high performance must consider the person as a whole. Executives are, in effect, "corporate athletes." If they are to perform at high levels over the long haul, they must train in the systematic, multilevel way that athletes do.

Rooted in two decades of work with world-class athletes, the integrated theory of performance management addresses the body, the emotions, the mind, and the spirit through a model the authors call the performance pyramid. At its foundation is physical well-being. Above that rest emotional health, then mental acuity, and, finally, a spiritual purpose. Each level profoundly influences the others, and all must be addressed together to avoid compromising performance. Rigorous exercise, for example, can produce a sense of emotional well-being, clearing the way for peak mental performance. Rituals that promote oscillation—the rhythmic expenditure and recovery of energy—link the levels of the pyramid and lead to the ideal performance state. The authors offer case studies of executives who have used the model to increase professional performance and improve the quality of their lives.

Oncken, William Jr., and Donald L. Wass. "Who's Got the Monkey?" *Harvard Business Review,* November–December 1999. Is a failure to delegate costing you time and energy? If it is, you must read this updated version of the classic 1974 article. It's timeless.

Many managers feel overwhelmed. They have too many problems—too many monkeys—on their backs. Often, they find themselves running out of time while their subordinates are running out of work. These authors tell an engaging story of an overburdened manager who has unwittingly taken on all of his subordinates' problems. The article is updated with special commentary by Stephen Covey.

von Hoffman, Constantine. "Getting Organized." *Harvard Management Update,* January 1998. Having trouble cutting through all the clutter around you? Need help with "pile management"? If you answered yes to either question, this short article can help you.

Although there is no single best method for organizing yourself, von Hoffman taps in to some perennially useful techniques to manage your disorganization. Through managing your space, organizing your schedule in collaboration with others, prioritizing your to-do list, and correctly filing things so that they remain accessible, you can reduce the hundreds of hours lost each year searching for lost items.

Index

About the Subject Adviser

MICHAEL ROBERTO is a faculty member in the General Management unit at the Harvard Business School. Professor Roberto's research focuses on strategic decision-making processes and senior management teams. He has published articles based upon his research in the *Harvard Business Review, California Management Review, Ivey Business Journal*, and *The Leadership Quarterly*. His research has examined how managers make strategic decisions in a timely and efficient manner while simultaneously building the consensus often required to implement decisions effectively.

Over the past few years, Professor Roberto has taught in the leadership development programs at a number of firms, including The Home Depot, Mars, Novartis, The World Bank, and Thales. He has also consulted with organizations such as Lockheed Martin, Corporate Executive Board, and Morgan Services.

Professor Roberto received an A.B. with honors from Harvard College in 1991. He earned an M.B.A. with High Distinction from Harvard Business School in 1995, graduating as a George F. Baker Scholar. He also received his D.B.A. from the Harvard Business School in 2000.

About the Writer

RICHARD LUECKE is the writer of many books in the Harvard Business Essentials series. Based in Salem, Massachusetts, Mr. Luecke has authored or developed more than forty books and dozens of articles on a wide range of business subjects. He has an M.B.A. from the University of St. Thomas. He can be reached at richard.luecke@verizon.net.

Harvard Business Review Paperback Series

The Harvard Business Review Paperback Series offers the best thinking on cutting-edge management ideas from the world's leading thinkers, researchers, and managers. Designed for leaders who believe in the power of ideas to change business, these books will be useful to managers at all levels of experience, but especially senior executives and general managers. In addition, this series is widely used in training and executive development programs.

Books are priced at $19.95 U.S.
Price subject to change.

Title	Product #
Harvard Business Review **Interviews with CEOs**	3294
Harvard Business Review on **Advances in Strategy**	8032
Harvard Business Review on **Becoming a High Performance Manager**	1296
Harvard Business Review on **Brand Management**	1445
Harvard Business Review on **Breakthrough Leadership**	8059
Harvard Business Review on **Breakthrough Thinking**	181X
Harvard Business Review on **Building Personal and Organizational Resilience**	2721
Harvard Business Review on **Business and the Environment**	2336
Harvard Business Review on **Change**	8842
Harvard Business Review on **Compensation**	701X
Harvard Business Review on **Corporate Ethics**	273X
Harvard Business Review on **Corporate Governance**	2379
Harvard Business Review on **Corporate Responsibility**	2748
Harvard Business Review on **Corporate Strategy**	1429
Harvard Business Review on **Crisis Management**	2352
Harvard Business Review on **Culture and Change**	8369
Harvard Business Review on **Customer Relationship Management**	6994
Harvard Business Review on **Decision Making**	5572
Harvard Business Review on **Effective Communication**	1437

Management Dilemmas: Case Studies from the Pages of Harvard Business Review

How often do you wish you could turn to a panel of experts to guide you through tough management situations? The Management Dilemmas series provides just that. Drawn from the pages of *Harvard Business Review,* each insightful volume poses several perplexing predicaments and shares the problem-solving wisdom of leading experts. Engagingly written, these solutions-oriented collections help managers make sound judgment calls when addressing everyday management dilemmas.

These books are priced at $19.95 U.S.
Price subject to change.

Title	Product #
Management Dilemmas: **When Change Comes Undone**	5038
Management Dilemmas: **When Good People Behave Badly**	5046
Management Dilemmas: **When Marketing Becomes a Minefield**	290X

Harvard Business Essentials

In the fast-paced world of business today, everyone needs a personal resource—a place to go for advice, coaching, background information, or answers. The Harvard Business Essentials series fits the bill. Concise and straightforward, these books provide highly practical advice for readers at all levels of experience. Whether you are a new manager interested in expanding your skills or an experienced executive looking to stay on top, these solution-oriented books give you the reliable tips and tools you need to improve your performance and get the job done. Harvard Business Essentials titles will quickly become your constant companions and trusted guides.

These books are priced at $19.95 U.S., except as noted.
Price subject to change.

Title	Product #
Harvard Business Essentials: **Negotiation**	1113
Harvard Business Essentials: **Managing Creativity and Innovation**	1121
Harvard Business Essentials: **Managing Change and Transition**	8741
Harvard Business Essentials: **Hiring and Keeping the Best People**	875X
Harvard Business Essentials: **Finance for Managers**	8768
Harvard Business Essentials: **Business Communication**	113X
Harvard Business Essentials: **Manager's Toolkit ($24.95)**	2896
Harvard Business Essentials: **Managing Projects Large and Small**	3213
Harvard Business Essentials: **Creating Teams with an Edge**	290X
Harvard Business Essentials: **Entrepreneur's Toolkit**	4368
Harvard Business Essentials: **Coaching and Mentoring**	435X
Harvard Business Essentials: **Crisis Management**	4376

The Results-Driven Manager

The Results-Driven Manager series collects timely articles from Harvard Management Update and Harvard Management Communication Letter to help senior to middle managers sharpen their skills, increase their effectiveness, and gain a competitive edge. Presented in a concise, accessible format to save managers valuable time, these books offer authoritative insights and techniques for improving job performance and achieving immediate results.

These books are priced at $14.95 U.S.
Price subject to change.